INDUSTRIAL FRUSTRATION

COMMONSENSE FOR TRADE UNIONISTS

INDUSTRIAL FRUSTRATION

COMMONSENSE FOR TRADE UNIONISTS

by

LEWIS C. ORD

With a Foreword by

SIR EDWARD PEACOCK

LONDON

THE MAYFLOWER PUBLISHING CO. LTD.

17 FARRINGDON STREET, E.C.4

FIRST PUBLISHED 1953

To Brian Sixsmith, who has understood and applied the principles of practical management with excellent results.

Set in Baskerville type and printed by
HENRY BURT AND SON LTD.
8-10 MILL STREET, BEDFORD

Made in Great Britain

CONTENTS

PUBLISHER'S NOTE

Lewis C. Ord died suddenly on 22nd June last, shortly after he had completed this book, but before he could see it in proof or had settled its title. He had it very much in his mind that the book should be read by Trade Unionists who would appreciate that the solution of Britain's industrial difficulties lies largely in their hands. The choice of title *Industrial Frustration*, with its sub-title *Commonsense for Trade Unionists*, is a reflection both of this thought and of the industrial impasse which is described in the book.

His death has deprived British industry of one of its outstanding minds; a man who saw more clearly than most of his contemporaries, not only the root causes of industrial decline, but, more important, the remedies.

Mr. Ord, a Canadian, was born in 1881. He received his early grounding in mass-production methods on the Canadian Pacific Railway and in the United States. In the first World War he commanded a Canadian battery in France. After it was over he turned his attention to industrial consulting, and advised and re-organised a number of major companies in England, France and Belgium. In 1938 he became consultant to the Air Ministry. Later he went to Australia at the request of the Australian Government to advise on aircraft production. During the second World War he became Director of Planning to the British Air Commission in the United States. On his return to this country he became consultant on methods of Government work to the Treasury and other departments.

He resumed his consulting work after the war and also became widely known as a lecturer on industrial subjects, a broadcaster, and writer. His books, *Secrets of Industry, Politics and Poverty*, and *Industrial Facts and Fallacies* form a contribution to industrial recovery completed by the present volume.

R.H.M.T.

January 1953.

FOREWORD

I knew Lewis Ord well when he was a schoolboy in Toronto over fifty years ago, and since then we have met from time to time and exchanged views on industry.

A well-trained Engineer, industrial management soon became his special interest, and for many years he deliberately moved from one job to another, in Canada, the United States and Great Britain, in order that he might become familiar with the best in these countries.

In later years he was an industrial consultant, and his advice was sought by many of the leading companies of Great Britain.

Ord made a notable contribution to industrial efficiency by his advice to these companies, and by his books and lectures on the subject. In this new volume which proved to be his last he restates his beliefs and applies them to the problem of larger and more efficient production, which is such a vital need of British industry today.

He believed in giving the men on the spot—the foremen and junior executives—power to make all decisions that can possibly be made without reference to higher authority. "The further the point at which work is planned, directed and controlled lies from the place where the work is done, and the less the power to make decisions lies with foremen and junior line executives, the larger would be the possible economies. The closer the planning and the direction of work is taken to the place where the work is done, the greater will be the economies effected by that change."

His views should be studied by all who have to do with this vital matter.

EDWARD PEACOCK

29th December 1952.

INDUSTRIAL FRUSTRATION

COMMONSENSE FOR TRADE UNIONISTS

CHAPTER I

INDUSTRIAL LEADERSHIP

AMERICAN METHODS

IN 1920 I had a hunch that a British Industrial revival relative to the United States was about to take place. It was long overdue. I had noticed a willingness to adopt new ideas that I believed indicated a general change in policy. I was so sure that a sharp improvement in British industrial methods and efficiency was about to occur, that I left a senior managerial position on the other side of the Atlantic to take part in it. My hunch was a bad one. By 1951 the American industrial lead over the British had doubled.

I had seen something of British industry. I had come over with the Canadian troops in 1915. Up to the armistice I spent most of my time in France. After the armistice I managed to have a good look at British industry. I was disturbed at much that I saw. Anyone with a thorough training in American industry would, in my opinion, have a great chance to make money in British industry. There were plenty of things which could be done more efficiently.

A large British company offered me a post as works manager not long after my return to Canada in 1919. I was to have a free hand to introduce American methods. I did not hesitate. I resigned my position and came to England.

There were no doubts in my mind. I believed I knew exactly what was necessary in order to make British industry in all respects as efficient as American. Line production, American managerial and production methods with adequate tools and equipment would do all that was necessary. Most Americans and Canadians thought the same.

This is not a personal history. Many Americans and Canadians during the last thirty years thought and acted as I did. They were among the most capable and experienced men who could have undertaken such work. They did all they knew to make the British factories under their charge as efficient as similar factories in the United States. They taught the staffs under them all they could about efficient production. In spite of all they were able to do, the American industrial lead steadily increased.

It is not true to say that British industrial efficiency had declined. It had risen. But American and Canadian industrial efficiency had risen twice as fast over the same period of time. The British public appeared both unaware of and unconcerned over the rapid rate at which the Americans were increasing their lead. When the fact was demonstrated to them on some point upon which there was no room for doubt, the general attitude was that the United States possessed physical and material assets which made her lead inevitable. They felt that lead would increase in the future.

AMERICAN METHODS IN BRITAIN

The British are a proud race. They have accepted this steadily increasing American industrial lead only because they believed it inevitable. There is nothing the average Briton likes less than continued dependence on American aid and advice. They have a guilty feeling about it because they suspect it is due largely to the relative British industrial decline which they have so far been unable to prevent.

Americans and Canadians are also concerned over this relative British decline. Both have helped with money and materials to enable Britain to get on her feet again. Both are poorer today than they would have been had Britain not needed their help. Canada in particular is suffering heavily from British inability to buy Canadian products, even when they cost less than similar products from any other country. British manufactured products, on the other hand, are not cheap enough to be sold abroad in sufficient quantities to provide the dollars Britain requires. This is, roughly, the story of the dollar gap.

Were British industry more efficient, this situation would not occur. In spite of wage rates about half the usual Canadian and American rates, British goods are, as a rule, too highly priced to sell in sufficient volume in Canadian and American markets. This is the clearest possible evidence of the lack of efficiency in British industry.

Americans have not confined themselves to giving good advice. They have realised that a practical demonstration of the degree of efficiency it is possible to achieve in British industry is preferable. Some of the most efficient of American firms have set up factories in this country with that object in view. If things had worked out as they hoped, there should have been plenty of money in it for them.

These ventures were managed by some of the most capable and experienced of Americans. Most of them had established reputations in similar jobs on the other side of the Atlantic. The equipment was worthy of the very efficient American firms backing the venture. Management and production methods were American. In spite of these advantages, only a percentage of these American owned and operated firms in Great Britain led their British competitors; these led by a narrow margin. Others did not lead. Americans have been unable to demonstrate that they can manage and operate businesses in Great Britain with markedly greater efficiency than their British rivals.

Individual Americans and Canadians had believed that American managerial and production methods were very superior to the British. In their opinion these had only to be demonstrated to win instant adoption. American and Canadian firms had the same conviction. Both put their beliefs to a practical test. None of these tests has proved American

3

managerial technique to be superior on average to British. The reasons for American industrial leadership lie in some other direction.

None of us were theorists. We all had had good managerial records in the United States and Canada. Most of us were working in the same industry we had worked in on the other side of the Atlantic. We knew our job thoroughly and in detail. We had all we believed necessary to enable us to achieve American levels of efficiency in British industry. The results were not up to our expectations. These factories operated at British and not at American levels of efficiency.

It was a lesson we all needed. Our theories, put to a practical test, did not work out. Much more was necessary before British industry could be made as efficient as American. We did not know what else was required.

It would be easy to misunderstand what is implied. As far as I know, we were all successful in what we came out to do. We managed the businesses we came to run very successfully, but we did not establish the superiority of our methods over the best of British management to the degree we had hoped and expected. We discovered we were not able to raise the efficiency of a British business to American levels in all respects.

In my own case, the improvement in the performance of the factory under my charge was spectacular. The firm was making a heavy loss when I took over. The profit made in the following year amounted to many hundreds of thousands of pounds. This was largely due, however, to the introduction of line production and the use of production tools and methods that were new in this country.

It was a very successful effort from a personal point of view. As an effort to make a British business as efficient in all respects as a similar business in the United States or Canada, it was a complete failure. It was probably operating more efficiently than any similar British plant. The overall man hour results fell far below what I had accomplished in a similar factory on the other side of the Atlantic.

4

Measuring the American Lead

It is not difficult to get a rough idea of the American lead in a particular industry. The one in which I was engaged was paying between 60 per cent and 70 per cent of American wage rates in 1920. In spite of that fact, its selling prices per pound or per ton in world markets were some 50 per cent above American. The situation in several other British industries was similar. A British industry today is not as efficient as its American opposite number when its selling prices in world markets are level. British wages at half American rates require that British selling prices should be far below American to show real equality in manufacturing efficiency.

These facts I know. I went to leading American business men to see if I could get from them the information I lacked. I was disappointed. Their ideas were the same as mine had been before I put them to a practical test. They were surprised at what I had to tell them. Most of them, on reflection, said they had sufficient personal knowledge of what happened to know that what I said must be true.

They excused their lack of knowledge both then and since. American business men have had a very strenuous time over the last twenty-five years. The great boom was followed by the great slump. Rearmament was followed by war, a boom, a minor slump and now by another boom based on rearmament. Usually their business had required all the attention they could give it, if it was to prosper. They had little need or time to study the conditions under which industry operated in other countries.

They did know what was necessary to make a business operate efficiently in the United States. Whether a business operated with exactly the same tools and by the same methods in Great Britain would achieve the same efficiency was something they had no means of knowing or finding out. What changes in the conditions under which industry operates in Great Britain would be necessary to ensure industrial efficiency at American levels was something they felt American business men could not be expected to know.

British business men whom I questioned, did not have the answers either. Their opinions differed widely. Some stoutly denied the existence of an American industrial lead, in spite of all the evidence to the contrary. Others acknowledged British industry was behind and dropping further behind. The remainder varied between the one extreme and the other.

They varied as widely in their suggested cures. One section put almost the whole of the blame on British working men. They said that they did not work hard enough. The more usual opinion was plainly American in its origin. Bigger companies, more standardisation and larger outputs of one unvarying product were the usual preliminary qualifications. Management and production on American lines backed by machines and power to drive them to American standards or better was what was needed. This, they believed, would bring the overall efficiency of British industry fully up to American levels.

It is not surprising that so many British business men shared these beliefs. This point of view had been pressed on them by Americans frequently and over a long period of time. It is not surprising that they accepted it as a full and complete explanation of the reasons for American industrial leadership. I was not able to get from British business leaders reasons for the continued British industrial decline which would bear careful examination.

There was another source of information open to me. I read many British, American and other books dealing with these subjects. They contained a great deal of factual, statistical and other information that was of value. They did not explain in a full and satisfactory manner the British industrial decline relative to the United States, how it came about or how to check it.

This was something I had determined to find out. I was unable to get satisfactory answers from the persons I thought would know, or from books. It appeared to me that the only way to get the information I wanted would be to dig it up for myself.

REASONS FOR THE AMERICAN LEAD

Finding out for myself I soon discovered to be a task of some magnitude. I would have to start afresh and to study the problem carefully and thoroughly. To do this I realised I must acquire a thorough comparative knowledge of both British and American industry. I hoped to be able to deduce correctly the reasons for the steadily increasing American industrial lead after I had collected the basic facts.

I secured positions successively as works manager, general manager, managing director and chairman of several British companies. My time limit was a maximum of two years in each post. In addition I held the post of general manager first in a Canadian and then in an American firm—again under two years in each post.

Consulting work in a number of companies, large and small, and in several countries, added to my experience. Several government departments have employed me as a consultant, both in this country and abroad. For some thirty years I devoted myself to the problem of finding out why America leads. I spared myself no effort to get the information I wanted.

The British are not a decadent race. In themselves and in their country, backed as it is by the Commonwealth and Empire, they possess everything they require to regain their old place as one of the world's industrial leaders. They lost their old leading position solely because they adopted some unsound social, industrial and economic ideas. The reasons for the American lead will be presented as simply and precisely as possible. They should be sufficient to show what Britain would require to do in order to regain her old position.

The British have on many occasions won the admiration of

the whole world. They show at their best when they are in a tight corner. They have never been in a tighter corner, industrially, than today. They would like to regain their former leading position in world affairs. Nothing would act with greater certainty to bring about that result, and a strengthening of the Commonwealth ties, than a British revival relative to the United States. This can be done with certainty and without using any new and untried theories. It can be done, without great capital expenditure or working longer hours, by increasing the labour force with persons drawn from unnecessary non productive posts. Because it is necessary for the future prosperity of the country, the Commonwealth and the Empire, I believe it will be done.

CHAPTER II

EARLY INDUSTRIAL DEVELOPMENTS

THE GREAT INDUSTRIAL REVOLUTION

BRITONS have reason to be proud of the great Industrial Revolution and the part their country and countrymen played in it. When it started, it was mainly a British affair. The basic inventions which set it under way were British. Even when the basic invention was American—the first steamship was built by Robert Fulton and ran on the Hudson River—the British developed the idea more rapidly.

New and improved tools, machines and methods, aided by steam power, increased production per head very rapidly. Over this same period, the population of Great Britain increased even more rapidly. Over the hundred years from 1814–1914 production per head rose to four times what it had been. The population grew to five times its former total. Private persons found the capital necessary to finance industrial expansion at this very rapid rate. In contrast the United States was handicapped by lack of capital in the early days of the industrial revolution.

It is now about 175 years since the United States of America was formed. It was then a poor country struggling to establish itself industrially, and trying to create homes for its people out of land that was then mainly undeveloped forests and plains. It was, relative to Europe, almost without class distinctions. The government was firmly in the hands of the ordinary folk.

Great Britain was a very different country 175 years ago. The countryside was well settled. Farms and hedges were neat and well tended. There were plenty of roads. It was obviously a land of advanced settlement and wealth. This was the period in which some of the largest and finest of British town houses and country mansions were built. The furniture and furnishings they contained cannot be duplicated today. They were made by hand by craftsmen of a skill that no longer exists.

The number and the size of those great houses with their attendant estates began to increase more rapidly about the time the Great Industrial Revolution got under way. Persons with wealth became very wealthy indeed. Land was wealth in those days and investments in industry increased that wealth. There were more persons engaged in domestic service of all sorts at that time than were employed in industry. High ranking officers of the government, the army, judges, senior civil servants and persons in prominent positions in the state usually occupied large houses and had many servants to wait on them. The ordinary folk were very poor. Class distinctions in British society were strongly marked. There was a great gulf between the upper and lower levels.

The various classes did not mix and the lines between them were strictly drawn. For example, members of the aristocracy and the landed gentry considered it beneath their dignity personally to engage in trade or industry. A classical education was still considered the best sort of education for a gentleman, almost regardless of the position he was destined to fill later in life.

As a direct result of this situation, almost all the early leaders of British industry were men of the people who had worked their way up, or who had been promoted from the ranks. In this particular, British and American industry started on very similar lines. Practical men remained in charge of industry for the whole of the period during which Britain led the rest of the world.

It is essential to a clear understanding of these early developments in British industry to realise how very poor were the wage earners relative to modern times, prior to the commencement of the industrial revolution. They wore homespun. As the name implies it was made at home. Almost everything they ate, wore or used was produced locally or made in the homes of the ordinary folk. Industry as it was before modern developments began existed almost entirely to meet the needs of the well to do, the navy, the army, the state, local authorities and similar bodies. The aggregate earnings and purchases of the masses were not sufficient to make any appreciable contribution towards keeping industry busy.

As industry developed, its output has gone more and more to meet the needs of the working classes. The needs, or more correctly, the orders on industry for the well to do have not risen at the same speed. Said differently, the expansion of industry and the rise in the standard of living of the poorer of the people are developments which occurred concurrently, the one dependent on the other.

Only in the southern American states were there large houses with large staffs of coloured servants run in British style. These states have tended to retain their basic British social and domestic customs which have, over the years, acquired a very attractive typically American character. In the rest of the country in the early days, men with money lived in less ostentatious style while workers in the north enjoyed a far better standard of living than workers in the south. Until very recently, the south has remained a backward area industrially relative to the rest of the country.

THE EARLY BRITISH LEAD

The British turned out more real wealth per head of the population than any other country for at least two thirds of the period after the Great Industrial Revolution started. They had the most efficient and best paid craftsmen. In spite of paying higher real wages than any other country, British manufactured goods were famous the world over for their relatively high quality and low price. London was the central money market of the world. British business men were more prosperous and wealthy than those of any other nation.

The British mercantile marine was as large as the combined shipping of several other countries. The navy was as large as the two next largest together. The Union Jack flew over nearly a quarter of the land area of the world and about one fifth of its population. With this great trading empire, Great Britain held commercial and industrial advantages greater than those of any other country.

The British have not usually been isolationist; when they were wealthy they lent a hand to other nations. British men, money and machines have helped to build up the industries of many other countries, including particularly the United States. They helped the other countries of the world along in another very valuable way. They permitted food, raw materials and manufactured goods to enter the country duty free. The principal exceptions to that rule were wines, spirits and tobacco. This encouraged other countries to sell their products in Great Britain. It gave them the currency with which to buy British manufactured goods.

This policy set a high standard of manufacturing efficiency for the British. They had to be able to make and sell goods at prices lower than similar goods could be imported from abroad. It kept prices in the British home markets lower than would have been possible on any other basis. There was far greater compulsion to efficiency in British industry at that time than in any other country.

It seems strange that as recently as 1880, Great Britain was well in front, the undisputed industrial leader of the world, with better industrial equipment and greater wealth than any other nation. No other country had done nearly as much industrial development work at home and abroad. If industrial developments in the future were to be on a wider and more intensive scale, then Great Britain was better provided than any other nation with the men, the money, machines and experience necessary. They were in the lead. They appeared to have everything that was necessary to enable them to increase that lead.

In the relatively short space of seventy years, Great Britain has dropped far behind the present leaders. Britain's industrial production per head is now scarcely half the American.

THE ORIGIN OF TRADE UNIONS

There have been organisations in industry to protect the interest of craftsmen for many years. These organisations were called guilds. Their members included not merely the craftsmen, but also their masters who were also craftsmen and worked beside their men in the small businesses of those days. Masters and men were both subject to the rules and strict discipline enforced by the guilds. Businesses grew bigger with the coming of the Great Industrial Revolution. The craftsmen in these businesses—not the men at the top—felt the need of some organisation to advance their interests and to protect them against unfair demands from their employers. The hours worked were too long and the working conditions were bad. Female and child labour were both used, and abused.

Modern trade unions were the result. This was another British development which soon spread to other countries in very similar form. It was unfortunate that successive British parliaments over a considerable period of years did not like the idea. They were convinced that these new organisations would do industry a great deal of harm. They passed laws making trade unions illegal. There were heavy penalties if these laws were disregarded.

British workers did their best under these handicaps, and a very good best it was. Without an organisation to direct their efforts and put organised weight behind their demands, they nevertheless managed to force British wage rates up faster than in any other country, including the United States. A great deal of bitterness, however, was created in the minds of trade unionists and workers by these unwise laws. In time they were repealed. The resentment they incurred continued to exist. British workers became convinced that they could not expect justice until they had a government of their own with workers at or near the top. Over the years they pressed constantly towards this goal. They achieved their objective.

When British trade unions were first formed they were not interested in politics. They did not pretend to consider the interests of any but their own members and workers generally. They saw to it that both got a fair share of the increased production of real wealth created largely by their own efforts. They insisted on and obtained shorter working hours and better working conditions in industry. They prevented victimisation. As far as their knowledge and power enabled them to do, they tried to maintain the conditions of full employment in their particular business or industry.

For the whole of the earlier part of the Great Industrial Revolution up to about 1880, British skilled craftsmen received the highest real wages in the world. No other workers were more skilled, more willing or turned out more per head. On average they enjoyed better working conditions than the workers of any other country, although similar conditions would be considered very poor today.

Higher real wages and better working conditions did not make British goods more expensive than those of any other country. In spite of the fact that manufactured goods and raw materials were allowed to enter Great Britain duty free, exports usually exceeded imports by hundreds of millions of pounds sterling each year. This is the period in which Great Britain built up her great investments abroad which stood her in such good stead in later years. British trade union action in these early days was not a handicap to manufacturing efficiency, as the results achieved demonstrated beyond doubt.

By comparison, the American trade unions got away to a bad start. Great hostility was directed against them, as a general rule, by the business men of that country. They were not able to raise wage rates as successfully as were the British unions. In later years, however, Congress increasingly took the side of the trade unions. Legislation has been passed which gives American trade unions better bargaining rights and greater protection against hostile managements than even British trade unions enjoy today. With these improved conditions the American trade unions have made more rapid progress than their British like numbers.

WHY BRITISH PROSPERITY ADVANCED RAPIDLY

As soon as the great industrial developments described got under way, workers, aided by machines and mechanical power began to turn out two or three times as much work as formerly. A little later, as a direct result of these changes, businesses began to run out of work in some particular area or industry. This produced serious unemployment and distress among the workers and their families. Riots followed. Mobs formed intent on destroying the new machines which they regarded as the cause of their misfortune.

Business men the world over have shown exceptional ability in building up business to supply any quantities of any particular product for which there was a maintained or rising demand. Given time for development, they have shown they were able to meet all requirements either by supplying the product wanted at a satisfactory rate, or by finding a satisfactory substitute. Where they have not done so well has been in their inability to create and maintain a demand sufficient to keep businesses and work people fully employed.

In the short term view, the interests of trade unions and of business men appear irreconcilable. The workers always want higher real wages. Business men seek to keep wages as low as they can contrive. There is little room for philanthropists in business. Business men have to be realists if they are to survive and be successful. British business men in the past and present have always opposed the demands of workers and later of trade unions for higher real wages as effectively as they were able to do.

Working men and trade unionists in the early days of the

Great Industrial Revolution were neither trained economists nor experienced business men. Yet they performed a vital economic function for the nation. Had they not driven the wages of the workers up as fast as they did, the Great Industrial Revolution must have crashed in a welter of mass unemployment before it got well under way. As the industries of the nation, due to the installation of machines with power to drive them, increased production per head, the workers increased their demands and so gave industry more work to do in supplying the growing purchasing power of the mass of the people.

There can be no doubt that the trade unions and the ordinary folk in both countries have between them brought about a social revolution as great as the industrial revolution which accompanied it and made it possible. The change is more marked in Great Britain for there the need for change was greater. There are relatively fewer wealthy persons today while the ordinary folk are much better off. The sick and the needy get help from the state. The unemployed are not left to fend for themselves. These are just and desirable changes.

British industry led American over the first two thirds of these developments mainly because the British workers and their trade unions kept the demands for goods and services of British industry high. British business men did the rest. Working pace was good because labour was relatively expensive to buy, and businesses very profitable. British businesses were better equipped with tools and labour saving devices than those of any other country. During this period American industrial workers did not do so well in forcing wage rates up. When work was scarce they moved West and settled on farms. Farm lands were free to anyone who cared for such work at that time. There was also plenty of employment for labour on farms and in the mines.

Why American Industry Overtook the British

In steadily increasing degree from 1880 onward, the American trade unions did a markedly better job for their workers.

They forced real wages and purchasing power up more rapidly than the British unions who became increasingly preoccupied with politics. American demand rose more rapidly than British, until today American purchasing power is more than double the British level per head. This in turn brought about a much more rapid rate of expansion in American industry. The demand was there. Industry expanded to meet the demand.

Labour was scarce in the United States over most of the earlier period, and particularly skilled labour. A man could homestead land from the state without payment. In other words free farm land was available to those who would work them. Labour was required in many other directions in this new country where so many new developments were under way. Therefore, because labour was scarce and expensive and skill was lacking, American industry began to rely more and more on machines and mechanical aids. In part this more rapid mechanical development was due to other reasons. It applied particularly to the manufacture of products that were difficult and required more mechanical equipment to make.

A wealthy nation does not buy the same goods and services in the same proportions as a poor one. Only a nation with very high purchasing power in the hands of the bulk of the population could buy all the necessities of life that Americans consume today and still have money left to buy motor cars, radios, television sets, refrigerators, vacuum cleaners and other luxury goods in the profusion which they do. Only a country with exceptionally high industrial efficiency could produce all those things at double the British rate, and in addition give military and economic aid on a vast scale to the rest of the world. On top of all this they are turning out military and other equipment for themselves at a higher rate per head than in any other country.

These obvious and easily proven facts warrant serious consideration. The people of Great Britain, including those who consider themselves experts on these subjects, should try to discover why it is that the United States of America is able to turn out so much more real wealth per head than the people of any European country. If they do this with the care and thoroughness that their own future prosperity and that of the nation warrants, they will find the difference springs mainly from a different way of thinking and consequent action. Great Britain can produce as much real wealth per head as the United States if the people and their leaders correct some of their mistaken ideas and tackle the job on the right lines.

Higher real wages, forced on American business men very much against their will since 1880, have been one of the principal advantages American industry has held over the British. This rising demand was almost the only reason why the overall capacity of American industry rose so much faster than the British. As labour was relatively scarce and expensive in the United States, that expansion in capacity had to take place, if it was to occur at all, mainly by raising the output per worker. That this was so is obvious enough when the existing situation is viewed realistically. A higher output per worker, as everyone knows, requires more and better machines and more power to drive them for the industrial workers of the nation. That is exactly what the United States has today.

Had British trade unions been as successful in forcing British wage rates up since 1880 as the American unions, had the British government been as successful in keeping prices low as the American government, then British purchasing power per head all the way from 1880 to date would have been as high as American. Had this occurred, then the capacity, the tools and equipment and the power per head used by British industry would have expanded as fast as in the United States.

Other things would have been necessary before British industrial efficiency would have reached American levels. British trade unions, instead of restricting output by slow pace and other restrictions, would instead have had to strive to

18

increase output by all the means in their power as American trade unions usually have done. The British government would have had to take steps at least as effective as the American government to maintain the conditions of sharp and unrestricted competition in industry, and to pass and enforce anti-trust laws as effectively as was done in the United States.

Of its very nature, Government is a necessity; but it is or can be made a most expensive luxury as well. Other things being equal, the nation that wastes the least of its manpower and woman power in the administrative posts and office staffs that are required to perform the functions of government, will be the most prosperous. The docility and orderliness of the British public, relative to American, results in their permitting more of government and direction to be imposed upon them than would be possible in the United States in normal times. This is another of the British handicaps which is not always sufficiently realised.

The capacity of industry will increase only as rapidly as the maintained demands made upon it. In other words it will expand only as fast as the rising purchasing power of the people compels it to do.

It is expensive to increase industrial capacity or efficiency. The latter is a change that is usually resisted by all ranks from the bottom to the top. Management always preaches the need for better pace, more consistent effort and greater efficiency in method on the part of the workers. It dislikes the suggestion that these ideas should be applied to office staffs and managers and that these staffs should be cut. The attitude of the workers is exactly the same. They do not like methods which speed up productive work. The maximum efficiency in a nation's industries can only be achieved by effective competition maintained consistently over a long period of years. There must be compulsion to efficiency in some effective form or efficiency will fall, over the years, to lower levels than in other nations where competition has been kept keen.

CHAPTER III

UNEMPLOYMENT

The Duty of Every Citizen

THE first duty of every citizen is to provide suitably for himself and those dependent on him. For this a job is necessary at least for most men. In a modern world this is the only way they can provide for themselves and their families.

Each man or woman is bound to try to retain his or her job, unless they have a better one in sight. As far as they are able, they are bound to resist action by their employers that would deprive them of their employment. The interests of the firm and the individual are sharply at variance on such occasions.

Workers will try to rally their friends or their union to their support whenever their job is threatened. They in turn will try to help others when their jobs are in danger. Action of this sort must be expected. It is likely to become more organised the longer a shortage of jobs lasts.

Men who act in this way are good citizens acting to the best of their knowledge and ability. Their duty to their dependents comes first. In such circumstances trade unions are likely to be more concerned about keeping their members in jobs than with industrial efficiency.

British trade unions have been lectured for years over their attitude and actions when jobs are scarce. These criticisms have had no noticeable effect. Increased industrial efficiency means the use of fewer men to turn out a given volume of work. Whenever jobs are really hard to get or to keep, workers must be expected to resist increased efficiency. They are likely to pull as far as they think safe in the opposite direction.

In war-time British trade unions have usually permitted changes to increase output per worker. They have stipulated a return to normal when peace came. Undoubtedly trade unions have kept more men in jobs when jobs were hard to get by slow pace and restrictive tactics.

Workers in Britain are not impressed by arguments that only increased efficiency, faster working pace and higher outputs per head lead to higher real wages. They know that in recent years some workers have received heavy wage increases in spite of lower outputs per worker. They would all like higher real wages. They regard full employment as being far more essential.

Unemployment pay does not reconcile workers to being laid off. They are not made happy by being told there is work for them in some other town. The great majority are married. There is a great shortage of houses. Their wages are not high enough to pay board in one town and maintain a family in another.

British workers will not agree to remove all restrictive practices and to join wholeheartedly in increasing production until they are satisfied on unemployment. They will be hard to convince that no matter how high output rises, the country can be made to consume all that is produced. They have been told that tale before. They have long memories.

They have been told to copy American industrial efficiency. They do not deny that American workers are better off. They merely point to eight million unemployed in the United States as late as 1938, and say they are not prepared to copy that. Once again in the autumn of 1949 the American unemployed were about $3\frac{1}{2}$ million. They would like prosperity at American levels, but only if full employment can be guaranteed.

British workers are logical. If full employment cannot be guaranteed at present British levels of efficiency, how could it be guaranteed with production per head at double that rate. So far they have not had a convincing and unevasive answer to their question.

Preventing Mass Unemployment

Unemployment is almost as old as history. It became more frequent after the commencement of the Industrial Revolution. That was inevitable. Machines with power to drive them enabled each worker to turn out very much more. Output exceeded purchasing power. Men were laid off, often in large numbers.

Wage increases over the years have increased the purchasing power of the ordinary folk. The demands of the government on industry have grown greater. These two between them have kept industry busy striving to increase output to meet a rising demand.

Americans have demonstrated that the production of goods and services at double the present British rate is possible with full employment. Production at that rate would not continue for long unless the purchasing power in the hands of the ordinary folk continued at rather more than double the British level. There is a direct connection between productive capacity and purchasing power. Unless purchasing power is kept high enough to keep industry on its toes producing to the limit of its capacity, there will be unemployment.

Let us assume that British production per head could be doubled within ten years. Actually it is possible if everyone did his or her full share and all the necessary steps were taken. As a supposition, were this to happen, real wages would also have to be doubled, in order to maintain full employment. It is essential that the country should be able to consume all that industry is able to produce and be eager to consume more.

Let us assume that to double purchasing power, an increase in wages was given in each year equal to a tenth of the wage rate paid in the starting year. By the end of the ten-year period money wage rates would have doubled. So also would real wages and purchasing power, but only if prices had not risen at all over the same period. If prices had risen, then the wage increases would have to be proportionately greater.

When the wage rates of the workers go up, the earnings of all other classes of the community follow suit, if a little later and sometimes considerably later. The trade unions provide the motive power which determines the rate at which the reward of all classes will rise. Too much credit is given to American business men for the greater prosperity which Americans enjoy. The principal credit should go to the American trade unions. Had the demand on British industry for goods and services risen as fast as in the United States since 1880, British business men would have met that demand with a rise in overall capacity and in output per head at least as great.

There are very few people in the world today who do not wish to work. The exceptions in the main are those who are too young, too old or too ill. The people want to work. The nation needs and can use all its people can produce. For their mutual benefit it is essential that the leaders of each nation ensure that all who wish to work can find a job.

It is significant that business men in those countries where real wages have been driven up fastest are the most prosperous. These also are the countries with the largest, best equipped and most efficient industries. These are benefits which must always flow from high real wages. Profits also must be relatively large before this can happen. The capital equipment of industry is expensive and is better provided out of profits rather than out of taxation. Profits must be on an adequate scale if a nation is to be among the industrial leaders.

It should be said bluntly that business men do not normally increase purchasing power. On the contrary they strive to keep wages as low and the prices of their particular products as high as they can contrive. They try to attract purchasing power away from their competitors' products to their own. The public must rely mainly on the trade unions, and to a lesser degree on the government, to push wage and salary rates up and to keep prices low and so maintain the conditions of full employment and rising prosperity.

Business men in particular have missed the value to them

of the normal function of trade unions. Business profits are highest in those countries where the trade unions have done the best job for their members. Sixty to seventy years ago British business men were convinced that their country could not consume all they could produce, and that the only possible market for their surplus capacity was abroad.

American trade unions have fostered the opposite policy, even if it was unconsciously. They expanded the home market and purchasing power at a very rapid rate. Most of the additional business done in the home markets of both countries over the last sixty years or more has been found for the business men of each nation by their trade unions. The enlarged purchasing power of the masses now absorbs most of the productive capacity of industry in consumer goods.

A DANGEROUS SITUATION

The success that has attended the efforts of some nations to raise the standard of living of the poorer of their people has created a dangerous situation. The ordinary folk of some of the poorer nations will not live contentedly and at peace while their rate of reward is anywhere from a third to a tenth of what similar American workers receive. They are now conscious that they could and ought to earn more.

The people of all nations, no matter how prosperous they may be today, believe that they should receive more in the future. They are dissatisfied with things as they are. They would like to see the rate of progress speeded up. This is a good sign and one that ought to be encouraged.

While all are confident that better is possible, there are wide differences of opinion as to the best means for accomplishing that desirable result. In the poorer and less well educated countries of the world, the evidences of great wealth exist alongside abject poverty. It is natural that the very poor in such countries should think that the quickest and best way of putting that situation right would be to take from the wealthy and give to the poor. It is on that belief that Communism has progressed.

Not merely Communism has progressed by promising things that are unattainable in the near future. Politicians of all parties too often promise jobs for all with more pay for less work. Frequently these promises are made by persons who have neither the knowledge nor the ability to do the things they promise so readily, and which they later forget without apology. Their promises are believed only because the poorer people are so desperately anxious to believe them. Some political promises made in recent times have no more substance than the pot of gold which is said to lie at the foot of the rainbow.

The working classes in the more backward countries live under intolerable conditions. This produces a dangerous situation in which Communism breeds like a plague. While Communism cannot cure their troubles, it promises to do so. Time and time again the only choice open to these folks is either a continuation of things as they are, or Communism. When in such circumstances they elect to try Communism, it should not cause surprise. Unfortunately these poor people do not realise that if they choose to try Communism, they will not be given another choice. They will never be allowed to try some other system should they later decide they did not like Communism.

It is not enough to criticise Communism. When the conditions are desperate in some country, Communism does not twiddle its thumbs, talk high ideals and let things run on as they are. It gets on with what it is out to do while the opposition is still thinking about it. Taking from the wealthy to give to the poor, which is usually the first move, wins over the masses who are still undecided as nothing else could do as effectively. Once that has been accomplished, the men at the head of the Communist movement in the country concerned take all the usual steps to make their rule absolute and permanent.

It is futile to try to stop the spread of Communism by armed force. It is right to check the use of force by Communists by even greater force, so as to discourage its spread by that means. Much more effective is a higher standard of living, a sound democratic system of government, adapted to the beliefs of the country concerned, with greater personal freedom. First the people must be reached and persuaded before the alternatives to Communism can be tried. Great national wealth carries with it a responsibility towards poorer nations that has not been sufficiently realised and acted on in the past.

POLICY CHANGES CAUSE BRITISH DECLINE

God helps those who help themselves. Americans are not in front because they are better men or have a better country. They lead because their trade union and governmental policies have been wiser. They lead because they have provided themselves with more and more up-to-date tools and equipment and drive it more nearly up to the limits of its capacity. Prosperity was forced on their business men by rising demand for goods and services, a situation which was brought about mainly by their trade unions.

Had the British unemployed between the two wars been used effectively, they could have raised the quantity and the quality of British industrial tools and equipment to American levels or higher. It was a missed opportunity for the nation as well as the workers. British industrial production from 1880 to 1939 was not low due to lack of tools—except in war time. It was low due mainly to the fact that they did not use to capacity the tools and men they had.

The first of the changes in policy which brought about the British industrial decline relative to the United States started about 1875. According to the Federation of British Industries and other authorities, price rings and trade associations were first formed in Britain about that time. This was the first step in a long campaign aimed at killing effective competition in industry, and of enabling prices to be raised and maintained by agreement. It was not a movement that reached widespread popularity all at once. British business men had to be persuaded. This movement has grown slowly over the years. The number of businesses in the various British trade associations is far greater today than ever before. So also is their power. The formation of trade associations has had the general support of all three political parties in the past.

The American movement toward forming Trusts as a means of achieving monopoly began about the same time. The aim of these trusts was to be able to raise and maintain prices at will, after they had broken or bought out their competitors. The means used to kill off competition was price cutting too fierce for the other businesses to stand—the exact opposite of the British method. These efforts had not got under way very far when Congress brought in the Sherman Act in 1890. This Act made monopolies and price raising by agreement illegal. Since then the American government has brought in several additional laws to strengthen their anti-trust legislation.

Not long after the first British trade association was formed the first employers federation was created. Its object was to slow up the pace at which wage rates were rising by means of collective effort on the part of the employees. As a result of both trade associations and employers' federations, British wage rates rose ever more slowly while prices rose faster. These were the objects for which these associations were formed. The ultimate result of this policy was the mass unemployment between the two great wars.

American trade unions have had much better support from both political parties in the United States, than the British trade unions have had. There is no British equivalent of the Wagner and other similar Acts in the United States. American trade unions still enjoy negotiating rights established under law that gave them advantages and legal protection in many particulars which British trade unions do not yet enjoy.

The major difference between British and American trade

unions is undoubtedly in their attitude to politics. Americans, and particularly American trade unionists, think that they do better when trade unions as an organisation do not ally themselves with any particular political party. Individual trade unionists vote as they like. American trade union leaders have given financial help and more material support to whatever political party at the time promised strongest support for current trade union aims. Due to wiser tactics by the American trade unions, the reward of American workers is at rather more than double the current British rate. All classes of the American people from the highest to the lowest have benefited from wise action by the American trade unions.

The mistakes in British trade union policy with their inevitable consequences have been described. There is no need to repeat them. A great deal of nonsense has been talked in British political and trade union circles to the effect that capitalism has failed. The low level of real wages between the two great wars and the mass unemployment that occurred at that time are put forward as proof of this statement. The argument is absurd. Trade unions are essentially a part of the capitalist system. This system cannot function efficiently unless the trade unions perform their function wisely and well. The low level of real wages and the mass unemployment between the two wars was not evidence of the failure of the capitalist system. It was the measure of the degree by which the trade union leaders of Great Britain failed in their duty to the workers and to the nation.

The capitalist system will give of its best only if it is driven to the limit of its capacity all the time. No matter how rapidly efficiency and output per head may rise, trade unions must see that the real wages of the workers and the demands made on industry rise sharply enough to ensure a constant effort to increase the total of production and to raise efficiency. There must also be keen competition so that the most efficient firms are rewarded by greater prosperity, and that the least efficient businesses die and are forgotten. Prosperity depends on the effectiveness of the competition to do better, to produce more, and in particular to produce more efficiently.

When the British trade unionists decided that capitalism was a failure and could not be made to work efficiently, they took the two steps which, more surely than any others, would be bound to make the system fail. They defaulted in their trade union responsibility of forcing wage rates up fast enough to keep the businesses of the nation and the workers in them fully employed. When mass unemployment resulted inevitably from their default, they made a bad situation worse by taking steps to lower industrial efficiency and to reduce the output per worker in order to try and keep more of their members in employment.

CHAPTER IV

MASS UNEMPLOYMENT

BOOM AND BUST IN THE U.S.A.

IT has been related that mass unemployment occurred in Great Britain mainly because the purchasing power in the home market had not been advanced year after year as rapidly as production per head had increased. In other words, the capacity of British industry to turn out work had grown steadily, but because purchasing power had been allowed to lag behind, industry was not given enough work to do. This occurred in steadily increasing degree between 1880 and 1913. Only the steady increase of exports over imports which took place over the same period, averted a national catastrophe. In other words the mass unemployment which would otherwise have occurred was exported.

The price of British manufactured goods rose sharply, relative to world market price levels, during the 1914–1918 war. British wage rates had risen sharply during that war. Owing to extravagance in manufacturing methods that grew up during wartime, particularly of peace-time products, prices had risen. As a result of this and other factors, the total of British exports fell, but the volume of imports rose sharply. When the sellers' market after the war ended, mass unemployment settled on the country like a blight. Instead of exporting mass unemployment as the country had done before the war, Great Britain was importing it on an extensive scale.

Mass unemployment came to the United States in a very different way. It began almost overnight. It did not grow slowly over the years due to a faulty wage policy as in Britain. Although the immediate cause was different, the attack was quite as severe as in Britain. In spite of all the American Government did and spent, they were no more successful in their efforts to cure mass unemployment than the British Government had been. Mass unemployment continued until war cured it for them. War is never a permanent cure.

The British attack of mass unemployment had begun about the end of 1921. One after another, most of the European countries other than Russia suffered the same misfortune. For a long time the soundness of the American industrial system seemed to make her immune from such an attack. Then at the end of the longest and most sustained period of rising prosperity that the United States had ever known, mass unemployment struck suddenly in the autumn of 1929.

The American indexes of national production and prosperity, which had been rising steadily since 1919, were still rising, and with increasing speed, throughout most of 1929. This created a wave of optimism which reached its peak in the summer of that year. The great majority of Americans felt that they were in for a period of increasing output and of rising prosperity that would continue for some years to come. This belief in even better times in the future resulted in the value of shares, of land, and of businesses rising to new high levels. These were not justified by current earnings or by any prospective earnings then in sight. Even boom conditions continuing for an extended period could not have justified some of the prices then ruling.

Fortunes were made on the Stock Exchange. It was almost impossible to go wrong, as the prices of practically all shares were going up. Spending was on an equally grand scale, particularly capital spending. New factories were being built and old ones extended. The building of hotels and places of entertainment had been undertaken on a boom basis. House building, and particularly the larger houses, went forward at great speed. Spending at such a rate stimulated all business activities and expansion, a great deal of it neither wise nor necessary. Prices soared upwards in one last spurt. Then the

31

crash came. Values fell faster than they had risen. Some wealthy persons became almost penniless overnight. Thousands of businesses failed. Banks became embarrassed. The government was forced to step in and support the banks to prevent an epidemic of bank failures throughout the country.

Capital appreciation is treated as income and is taxed as income in the United States. During the boom in the summer of 1929 capital appreciation had added large and unreal amounts to the purchasing power of the American public. This unsound rise in purchasing power had induced heavy spending, and particularly capital spending. When the crash came, falling capital values reduced the total of the national income and purchasing power in far greater degree than they had previously inflated them. Serious losses to individuals and to businesses caused both to retrench. Wealthy persons who had taken part in the speculation were hardest hit. They reduced their own consumer spending to the lowest possible levels. Capital spending by individuals and by businesses was cancelled in some cases, and heavily reduced in others.

The owners and managers of American businesses have always been the nation's paymasters. The well to do who had speculated were forced to retrench. Businesses followed suit. Capital and consumer spending dropped sharply. Businesses started to cut pay rolls. Unemployment had reached the masses.

Working hours were shortened first. Overtime was cut out. Wage and salary cuts were made, usually by means of reclassification. Men were laid off. The purchasing power of the nation fell, not only due to men being laid off, but even more to the many other changes that reduced the take-home pay. The effect of these cuts in orders placed and in purchasing power, hit some firms very heavily at first. The necessity to retrench soon spread to the others.

The stocks of goods carried by warehousemen, wholesalers and shopkeepers toward the end of 1929 were very large. They had been built up in the expectation of a bigger business turnover and higher prices in the future. So long as these stocks lasted, the amount of mass unemployment was greater than it otherwise would have been. Businesses lived on them for as long as they could. This brought about a sharp reduction in the volume of orders placed with manufacturers. Manufacturers were therefore forced to lay off work people and staff. These changes further reduced the purchasing power of the nation.

Wholesalers and retailers did not buy, because their stocks were too large and the public were not buying. Wealthy people did not buy because times were bad; they were waiting for prices to fall to even lower levels, and then to start to rise, before they would buy. The masses did not buy because they did not have the money.

There were American business men who foresaw the consequence of severe retrenchment if persisted in for any considerable length of time. They tried to keep the volume of business done from falling. Many of them kept their businesses going on full volume. The small quantity of orders received soon forced them to cut staffs, reduce output and fall in line with the rest. For three years in succession the purchasing power in the hands of ordinary folk fell to still lower levels. The total of unemployed continued to rise.

It is true that the number of unemployed grew larger ever more slowly over the first three or four years of the depression. From then on the number of unemployed grew less, but again very slowly. In spite of all that the government and a number of far-sighted firms and business men were able to do, they found it impossible to restore confidence and normal output in American industry. Full employment was not achieved until 1942 when military service competed with industry for manpower.

PUMP PRIMING

The methods the American government first used in an effort to cure mass unemployment was termed "pump priming". It was felt that if the government gave industry enough work to do in one fashion or another, the added total of spending would, in time, increase the volume of business done to where the government's efforts might be discontinued and industry be able to carry on from that point under normal conditions. Unfortunately the expenditure that the government made for this purpose, great as it was, was not nearly enough to bring about a return to normal. The amounts of money spent were so vast, and the results achieved relatively so trifling, that the government despaired of achieving full employment on any such basis.

They therefore changed their policy from one of spending money to keep business busy, to one of helping individuals. It was found that more persons could be helped for a given amount of money spent, if it were used to give individuals a job. It was not direct charity as a rule. It was mainly payment for work done on building national highways, national parks and other works of national importance. It was found that money spent on big business projects hung fire for a long time before there was any material increase in the number of persons at work. Direct help to individuals on national projects was found not only to relieve more persons, but to effect the relief more speedily.

American business men attempted little and did little to cure mass unemployment. In the main they sat back and criticised the government. They had some justification for their complaints as the government were unable to accomplish in full what they had undertaken to do. Regardless of this however, the mess was one which the business men of the nation had created for themselves, mainly by speculation and over confidence. This is the important fact; it is too often overlooked.

In general, American business men resent government interference in industry in any form. When mass unemployment occurred, this, they felt, was an exception. They believed that the task of curing mass unemployment was beyond them, even if they had known exactly what to do, which they certainly did not. The general attitude of the American public is that the government should keep out of the day to day conduct of business in normal times. When some national emergency occurs which makes government intervention necessary, their preference is that the government should intervene to the smallest degree that will serve the needs of the particular case and that the government should get out as soon as their job is done.

Pump priming had cost the American government vast sums of money. It prevented a complete financial and industrial collapse. It was a necessary and unavoidable action. Direct assistance spending did improve the lot of millions. British and French spending on rearmament within the United States in 1938 and 1939 helped recovery along. American rearmament and Lend Lease during the following two years drove employment levels higher. Yet unemployment in many parts of the United States was serious in 1940 and even in 1941. It was not until after Pearl Harbour that full employment was achieved.

CAPITAL APPRECIATION

Low wage rates were not basically the cause of mass unemployment in the United States in 1929. The boom conditions were caused by capital appreciation and capital spending added to wage, salary and profit rates that were not too high. This capital appreciation added large and unreal amounts to the income and purchasing power of the nation. When the slump came, capital depreciation depleted the national income much more rapidly than it had previously raised it. The sharp drop in capital spending reduced the rate of national spending by a very serious amount. The purchasing power of the people, no longer inflated by capital values that were rising too fast, and seriously depleted by a rapid rate of capital depreciation, was no longer capable of maintaining employment at its former level, or anywhere near it. Mass unemployment became inevitable.

Perhaps a better way to explain to persons not familiar with the United States and their business habits at that time would be to compare what happened in the United States in 1929 and after with what happened to Great Britain in 1920 and 1921. The profits from speculation, from rising capital values and from tremendous capital spending in the United States up to the summer of 1929 had an effect similar to that of government spending in wartime, but with one important difference. There was no shortage of consumer goods in the U.S.A. in 1929 due to wartime requirements. In fact there was heavy overstocking of all these things in the expectation of still higher prices and heavier buying in the future. When the great additions to the nation's income by rising values was replaced by heavy falls, the fall in employment was heavy and immediate. It was as if heavy government wartime spending had ceased almost overnight. There was no cushion of post-war demand which kept British industry busy for two or more years after the war ended in 1918.

The only way in which mass unemployment in the United States in 1929 could have been cured at a profit—in contrast to the methods which were used which cost the national treasury vast sums of money and which were not successful—would have been by raising real wages. That is the normal method by which full employment or near it is maintained, in spite of the steady increase in the capacity and the efficiency of industry. This does not normally require great outlays of money by the state. It is profitable to both workers and business men, and consequently to the state as well.

WAGE INCREASES AND FULL EMPLOYMENT

The only method by which the workers and the ordinary folk of any nation can be given their full share of the increased production per head which occurred in the previous year is by increased wage levels. If there were no price increases, their wage levels should rise by the percentage by which productivity had increased in the previous year. If there had been price increases, then the wage increases would have to be proportionately greater to ensure that manual workers and other wage earners got their full share of the additional real wealth created by their efforts.

It is not intended to suggest that these wage increases should be by an equal percentage in all businesses and in all industries. One of the greatest of American industrial advantages is that they do not negotiate wage increases on a national basis, but business by business. The most profitable businesses and the most profitable industries are those which can best afford and are usually made to pay the largest increases. The differing wage scales which result help to draw workers away from the less efficient firms and declining industries to those that are more efficient, growing faster and in need of additional workers.

Should any company be forced to grant a wage increase to its workers without any increase in the selling price of its products, it is clear that its ratio of profit would fall at the time the increase was given. If the rate of increase in workers' wages throughout the country is by the same percentage as the productivity of industry rises in the same year, then for goods produced within the country no average rise in selling prices should be necessary. If the percentage of increased efficiency in the individual company was up to the national average increase year by year, then as a rule no increase in selling price should be necessary for that company due to such a wage increase. By the end of an elapsed year, the ratio of profit should have risen once more to its former percentage, assuming always that it continues to buy its materials, goods and services at the same prices as before.

The statements made in the paragraph above will not hold true unless the tax level and the demands made on industry by the state remain unchanged. The object of wage increases should be to ensure full employment and to give the workers their full share of the additional consumable real wealth produced each year by the increase in productivity of industry. Several acts by the state could render these wage increases unnecessary and even harmful. A heavy call up for the armed forces might so reduce the productive manpower of the nation as to make it inevitable that a fall in the total of consumer goods produced for civilian use must occur. In such a case a rise in purchasing power would be unnecessary and would do more harm than good.

There are other steps which the state might take which would make yearly real wage increases not merely unnecessary for the purpose of maintaining full employment, but definitely harmful. If the state made heavy demands on industry for capital goods or for equipment for the armed forces in times of full employment, the amount of consumer goods must fall proportionately to the degree to which manufacturing capacity had to be diverted to manufacturing for the state. There would then be fewer consumer goods available. Increasing purchasing power in the hands of the people would inevitably send prices up and do more harm than good. Fewer goods would be available for the public to buy. Purchasing power should therefore be reduced by taxation or by some other means in such circumstances.

Any gift of free services to the people by the state in times of full employment must be accompanied by a proportionate reduction in the total of real wages paid out to the workers. In no national sense is the service free. It must be paid for by the state. By whatever degree the state spends more for any purpose, the people must spend less. It all comes out of the total of national production.

If there is full employment, this total cannot be expanded save by the normal methods of slowly improving the efficiency of industry and by additions to manufacturing capacity or by expanding industry. When the state absorbs any of this capacity for any purpose, there will remain less available for the public. The amount of state spending is so great today that its effect must not be overlooked, even in the matter of yearly wage increases. When workers press for additional social services on a great national scale, they must be made to realise that they will have to forego wage increases to pay for them.

Pump priming as it was practised by the American Government in the period between 1929 and 1939 was an attempt to restore full normal conditions of business prosperity by a short and relatively small amount of government spending. Success in this attempt would have required government spending several times as large as was actually the case. Moreover that spending would have had to remain on a permanent basis until real wages, salaries and profits increased by a total at least as large as the total of additional government spending so as fully to replace it. If this be true, then it is clear that a more rapid rise of purchasing power of the workers and the ordinary folk was the basic need. It would have functioned best spread over two or three years or even longer; it should have been supplemented by increased state spending to whatever degree might have been necessary to make up the required total of purchasing power until it produced full employment.

Actually the American Government and people were shocked by the vast amounts of money that were spent by the state in pump priming on the one hand, and were alarmed by the degree to which the results achieved failed to restore anything like full employment and normal business conditions on the other. Their experience proved that pump priming was a costly and ineffective means of trying to restore full employment.

The main responsibility of ensuring that the workers and the ordinary folk of the nation consume enough goods and services to keep industry fully employed falls on the trade unions. No other body exists that can step in and raise the purchasing power of the masses sufficiently to ensure full employment or something near it. Jealous of their privileges and responsibilities, the trade unions would not permit any other body to interfere in duties they have made so exclusively their own.

To ensure full employment, it is not only necessary that the rate per hour be high enough; it is equally necessary that the total of hours worked, including overtime, be great enough to ensure that the take-home money is sufficient to buy goods and services enough to keep industry fully employed. If the wage increases granted in a year were exactly the percentage by which productivity had increased over the previous year, this would divide the additional yearly production of real wealth between capital and labour on exactly the same basis as in the previous year. This would hold true, however, only if there was no average price increase for the nation as a whole. If there were price increases, then profits would get more than their fair percentage of the increase.

There is another way in which full employment may be ensured—increased spending by the state. This merely means the state spending money the people might prefer to have and to spend for themselves. It does not matter whether the state spends additional money on pump priming, rearmament or social services, whether they do it to maintain full employment or for any other reason. By whatever amount the state spends more, the people must spend less. The total production of real wealth by a nation, when there is full employment, is not elastic. It cannot be stretched in any material degree just because the state has in hand projects it believes are worthwhile. The more the state takes, the less there is available for the people.

CHAPTER V

WORKING PACE AND INCENTIVES

THE PSYCHOLOGICAL APPROACH

THE older men in British industry have heard more about the need for greater incentives for working men over the last ten years, than in the rest of their lifetime. Industrial psychologists and a number of well meaning organisations have been very busy putting forward new views on this very old subject. Industrial consultants, university professors, politicians and others have taken a similar line. The ideas of these people as to how the job should be tackled have differed in detail. The general conclusion reached appears to be that they do not think British working pace, which they realise is slower than it ought to be, can be raised to higher levels without increased incentives.

They have other suggestions which they believe would assist in the attainment of this objective. Personnel management is an addition they strongly recommend. Another technique of handling men which they recommend is joint consultation in industry. The employment of industrial psychologists is a third. It is unfortunate that so many of these recommendations are made by persons without practical experience in industry—particularly in its lower ranks.

These ideas have not merely been talked about. They have been tried out very extensively over the last ten years, notably in the nationalised industries. The results are not up to expectation. Most practical business men would agree that working pace in British industry in 1951 was not as good on average as it was in 1938. Many think, and the evidence supports their belief, that these new ideas have done more harm than good.

It is unfortunate that the people responsible for these new ideas to improve working pace did not first take the trouble to find out where working pace is slowest and why it is slow. Working pace is a big problem to tackle. A great deal of factual information must first be collected before the problem can be viewed with reasonable accuracy and a cure prescribed. Many of the academic analyses are very wide of the mark both in what is wrong and in how to cure it.

Working pace varies considerably between similar businesses in the same industry and in the same country, even when tools, physical working conditions and incentives paid are closely similar. There are some parts of the same country where working pace is faster and other parts where it is slower than the national average. Working pace in some countries is considerably faster than in others. These are established facts. The first need is a knowledge that these variations in working pace do occur. The second is to know accurately why they occur. Then only is it possible to suggest a cure that really would work.

There are other variations in working pace which are equally in need of explanation. Some large British companies using piecework have found to their surprise that the piece-work prices paid for exactly the same job using the same tools and methods is often higher in their large factories than in their smaller ones. In American factories this tendency, although slight, is in the opposite direction. It would be possible to fill several chapters with other examples of variations in working pace that do occur in industry. For the general reader this would be boring, nor is it necessary for a clear understanding of the general problem.

Individual piecework is the principal suggestion for improving working pace in British industry. It is a strange suggestion considering that the United States, where piecework was once almost universal, is now dropping it. The garment workers, boots and shoes and some parts of the textile industry are among the few exceptions where individual piecework is still the vogue in American industry.

During the recent war I managed an American armament factory for a time for the sake of the experience. This enabled me to re-establish contacts with old business friends who were by then at or near the top of some large American businesses. Most of them, like myself, had been strong advocates of individual piecework in former days. I asked them if they liked the fact that piecework had been dropped under pressure by the American trade unions, and whether working pace and production costs were as satisfactory on the new methods.

Their answers surprised me. They were not anxious to go back to piecework. When the American trade unions forced them to drop piecework they found that the cost of setting and administering piecework had been far greater than they had realised. The dropping of this staff made an economy of some magnitude. It went a long way towards ensuring them against any loss that might have occurred through slower working pace. They all felt, however, that the drop in pace, if any, had been small.

There was another and greater gain when piecework was thrown out. At least three quarters of the disputes between management and workers disappeared. It is too often forgotten that setting a piecework price is settling a new wage agreement as far as the individual worker doing the job is concerned. The discussion is often acrimonious. On daywork all these unpleasant discussions and arguments disappeared. This was a clear gain for the managements concerned.

Considering all the various points, none of the practical men with whom I discussed the matter wished to return to piecework, even if the trade unions concerned would agree. Practical experience with both systems over a number of years had forced them to the conclusion that they were better off without it.

It is unfortunate that so much of the so called research into working pace in industry has been carried out by persons with a good academic background, but without practical experi-

43

ence in industry. A university education is not the best means of finding out what ordinary workmen think or why they think it. One of the declared objectives of university education in Great Britain is to change a man's way of thinking and to give him a new set of values, a different outlook on life and a different way of expressing himself. Education on these lines does not make it easier to understand a workman's aims and aspirations. It makes that task more difficult.

The lack of practical experience in industry, particularly of working beside working men in shop or factory doing the same work under the same conditions, deprives them of an experience that is vital to a sound understanding of this problem. Experience in handling men and in getting work done, both as foreman and as manager, is also required before any man can expect to understand this difficult problem. In fact it is better to have experience in several companies and in several countries. This would assist in understanding not only the variation in pace that occurs in the same country, but also between countries.

WHERE WORKING PACE VARIES

Some of the places where working pace varies have been mentioned earlier in this chapter. For some reason working pace in Great Britain is usually faster in industrial than in country districts. Working pace in some industrial districts is faster than in others. These considerable differences in working pace cannot be explained by differences in the rate of monetary reward or incentive. In the majority of the cases those differences in pace occur even where the rates of reward and methods of payment are the same.

When I was a young man, workers of many different European nationalities emigrated to the United States and Canada. Men of the same speech and race tended to live and work together. Most of the workers in one factory might be French, German, English or Polish. Other factories were manned almost entirely by native-born American or Canadian workers. There were hot arguments as to which of these various races worked best.

The relative working pace of men of these different nationalities was an important matter for some of the larger companies, and among them the railroads. About this time it was decided to standardise the charge for making repairs to the freight cars of the various railway companies when they were on other companies' lines. I was a member of the committee which dealt with this subject for the Master Car Builders' Association. We learned a great deal about the variation in working pace that exists between men of different races in the extensive investigations undertaken to establish these prices.

It is now generally accepted in the United States that the potential productive capacity of men of the Northern European races is equal to that of native born Americans or Canadians. The pace of European emigrants is always slower than that of native born American workers when they first reach the country. Most of the workers from continental Europe, on arrival, are slower in pace than newly arrived English or Scottish workers. All acquire the pace usual to the country and the district or trade in which they work, usually within a year.

When workers from some other country continued to work in groups consisting entirely of their own nationals it was observed that they took longer to become acclimatised and to adopt American pace. Where immigrants from European countries were mixed in with predominantly American born workers, the speed with which they adopted the American way of life and work was noticeably much more rapid.

The individual capacity of men of the same or of different races to turn out work varies considerably. How great are these differences the average research worker would never know—and for several reasons. The principal reason is that in an average British business they are not allowed to show.

There are some jobs on machines where the output of the

best worker will be very little greater than that of the poorest. Work which requires considerable physical effort and stamina combined with skill would show that some workers would turn out very much more than others if all worked to the top of their natural bent. In such circumstances the best worker in a factory or other group might turn out as much as double the poorest worker or workers in the same factory. That would be an extreme case. Usually differences would be smaller. The fact remains, however, that considerable differences in output per worker are usually not allowed to appear. The best worker would slow his pace until he was doing very little better than the rest.

An active and capable foreman would do his best to prevent great differences in individual output from appearing, but for different reasons. Workers who do badly on one job will often do particularly well on some other job they like and to which they are better adapted. Square pegs in round holes is something a good foreman will do his best to prevent.

For these and other reasons the individual variations in working pace and output of men in the same factory usually are not great. Men are picked for their suitability for a particular job. They are shifted about until the foreman finds where they work best. In fact the uniformity of piecework earnings in most British factories is always a surprise to persons who know the degree to which the individual capacity to turn out work varies.

Different shops or large groups in the same factory (not individuals) will often earn widely different piecework bonuses from other groups in the same factory. For example the paint shop workers may earn an average bonus each of 75 per cent over day rate. The sheet metal shop may earn 50 per cent and the machine shop an average bonus of 35 per cent. By way of contrast, the uniformity of the average earnings of the individuals in each of these groups is remarkable. This uniformity of output between individual workers in the same shop or group is not natural. It is wholly artificial. It is a uniformity created in the main by the workers themselves. These are important facts which must be known before the subject of working pace and incentives can be dealt with on a basis of reality.

WHY PACE VARIES

Piecework setting, including time and motion study, is not an exact science as far as new work is concerned. There are several reasons. In the first place the new price is not set by exact calculation; bargaining with the workers is necessary in an average piecework shop before the proposed price can be agreed. Trade union pressure usually results in some of the prices at least being set higher in the first place than they should have been.

No matter how correctly the time for the new job was estimated and the price agreed in the first place, there are few new jobs that should not be done considerably more quickly at the end of a two-year period. The operator acquires more skill and dexterity at the job. The material may be changed in several small details for the same purpose. Several small changes in tools, fixtures and methods may be made to save time or effort. None of these changes made one at a time may have been great enough to justify a request for a change in the piecework price. Taken in aggregate over a two-year period they may justify an increase in output of 25 per cent to 50 per cent and in a few cases even more.

In the average British shop where piecework is the rule, such a piecework price as has been described would remain unchanged at the end of two years. The output rate of the worker would also remain unchanged. This is one of the cases where piecework retards output. There are few engineering works using piecework that do not have many cases of this sort.

Incentives operate in reverse in the case mentioned above. In most British factories using piecework, working pace is slowest on those jobs where the possible earnings are highest.

Put differently, set the price of any job higher than normal as an inducement to the worker to turn out more work, and it will have exactly the opposite effect. The worker will earn no more money than he would have done on a somewhat lower price, but he will turn out less work. In other words increased incentive would result in a slower working pace.

These are things almost every piecework setter and practical foreman knows. It is something theorists who urge greater incentives in industry do not. The national campaign undertaken to increase the amount of individual piecework used in British industry has little justification. On American experience, it is a step backwards.

INDIVIDUAL VARIATIONS

Other things make working pace vary. Some individuals move and work naturally more quickly than others. Skill, dexterity, physical strength and endurance vary considerably. These factors taken together would make individual earnings on piecework vary widely did not the workers themselves take a hand to prevent wide variation.

Piecework setting of prices is not as uniformly accurate as those responsible for such work would have us believe. Their estimate of how long a job should take does vary in accuracy. Add the fact that all prices must be settled by bargaining with the workers. In such conditions some of the prices agreed will inevitably be set too high. Prices that are too low are always increased whenever it is demonstrated that the job cannot be done in the time allowed.

These various factors should result in very wide variations in individual piecework earnings, particularly in engineering shops. If all worked at their full normal pace there would be considerable differences in piecework earnings. Many accountants regard the uniformity of individual earnings that exists in most piecework shops as clear evidence of efficiency in production. It is evidence to the contrary. Men in such a shop produce uniformity by slowing the pace of the best workmen and of workers on jobs where the price was set too high to the pace of the slowest, so that the earnings of all would be relatively level. This is a normal condition with British piecework.

It has been mentioned that piecework survives in the United States in the textile industry and in boots and shoes. These are very suitable industries for the use of piecework. Many of the remarks made in the preceding paragraphs would not apply to these particular industries, if the piecework prices were set in an efficient manner. The garment industry is another in which piecework is still used and for which it is particularly suitable.

Where progressive improvements in the manufacture of a particular product are possible, piecework is often very unsatisfactory. Where the machines and the technique used can not be varied, and the only improvement that can be made depends on the skill and speed of the operator, individual piecework can be made to give very satisfactory results. Even in such cases, however, American experience is that group piecework or bonuses often work better and certainly will cost less to administer. Straight daywork, with or without an output bonus of some sort, is often better—particularly if the day work earnings are not far below the usual earnings on piecework.

Climate affects working pace. I remember the case of a factory in Georgia doing the same work by the same methods as one in Ohio owned by the same firm. This was a number of years ago when piecework set by the same methods was used in both factories. The times allowed for the same work were considerably longer for Georgia in the deep south than in the case of Ohio in the north. On heavy work the time differential was greater than for light work. Even office work suffered, output being lower in the south. This has brought about a considerable amount of air conditioning in factories built in the south in recent years.

49

NATIONAL VARIATIONS

It is well known that average working pace in the United States is faster than in Great Britain. British working pace, on the other hand, is faster than in most of the countries of Continental Europe. Experiments have been made by paying higher monetary incentives to raise both British and Continental European working pace to American levels. All these tests, and there have been many, failed. Monetary reward is not the principal reason for these national differences in working pace. Had it been, increased monetary reward would have cured it.

Working pace is not uniform throughout the United States even in the same industry. It is well known that working pace is slower in the building industry in New York, and that building costs are higher there than in the rest of the country. This is the case in spite of the fact that wage rates in the building trade in New York are higher than in the rest of the country. This is yet another case of monetary incentives working in reverse, and of pace being slowest where the reward is highest.

There are similar cases in Great Britain. The increase in wages rates granted to the miners over the last twelve years is greater than for any other similar group in the country. Hundreds of millions have been spent on new and improved capital equipment for the mines. In spite of all this additional mechanical aid and greatly increased wage incentives, the output of coal per miner in the latter part of 1950 was just slowly crawling back to what it had been in 1938. This is yet another case of higher monetary incentives resulting in slower working pace. Anyone with a wide experience in industry could mention other cases of the same sort.

There are industrial areas in France and in Belgium with incentives the same as for the rest of the country, where pace is slower. There are a few cases in each country where, in spite of higher wage rates, working pace is noticeably slower. There are some industries in each country where working pace is noticeably slower than in others. In some cases pace is best in the better paid industries. Sometimes it is the other way about. Much more evidence on the same subject could be presented, were it necessary to prove that there exist wide differences in working pace. Extensive tests show it cannot be cured by increasing the incentive. It would be a waste of money that might easily make the situation worse instead of better. A different and more informed approach to this problem is advisable.

There is yet another variation in working pace which occurs between businesses in the same country, in the same industry and in the same local area. These differences are sometimes considerable, varying from five to ten per cent above the average for that industry and district, to five or ten per cent below normal. Greater differences are occasionally experienced, mainly downward. In an earlier book, "Secrets of Industry" some interesting examples of these types of variations and their cure were given.

These variations are due to the variations in the quality of the supervision between one firm and another. It is mainly the foreman, and not the more senior management, that determine how well men will work in any firm, British or American. The firm that picks the best foreman, trains them in their own company methods on their own premises, and backs them best when they are on the job will always have the best working pace.

The commonest mistake made in British industry is in senior management dealing direct with the workers, particularly on matters of company policy and day to day matters arising from it. To the average worker, the foreman is the management. Working pace is best where the standing, knowledge and authority of foreman is best maintained by those above them. One of the worst situations occur when personnel managers and senior management generally deal with the workers direct without the foreman being present. What is even worse is where senior management in dealing with the workers make it apparent that the foremen are not fully informed on matters of company policy and are not permitted to deal with the workers on day to day matters without considerable guidance and overruling from above.

Men selected from the ranks for their character and their knowledge of the work and properly trained for that job by their company make the best foremen. Between different companies in the same industry, country and district, differences in working pace will not usually be due to a difference in the level of incentive or even to the type of monetary incentive used. Men will work best under the type of management and kind of men they like best. Of these, the foreman will matter most. They contact him more than anyone else. It is the foreman who makes him like or dislike his work, working conditions and the company for which he works.

Said differently, well selected and well trained foremen, fully acquainted with all matters of company policy that affect them or the workers, effectively supported by the senior members of the management team, can yield a company a dividend in the improved working pace equal to from five to ten per cent above the average for their industry and district. This is a result that cannot be made to come quickly. It takes years rather than months fully to win the confidence and the esteem of the workers. From a business and from a humanitarian point of view it pays for the trouble it takes. Happier men do more and better work.

Discipline is necessary in industry and is welcomed by the workers themselves. Put differently they dislike an absence of proper factory discipline. They do not like to work in a shop where bad workmanship, bad working pace, lateness and absenteeism escape without effective comment or punishment. Military discipline in a workshop would do much more harm than good. The discipline in a workshop where the best working pace obtains is rather that of a happy family where, to keep it happy, wrongdoing is punished.

One other rule is true today as it was in the time of Solomon.

52

A man should not be asked to serve two masters. That is a rule that is broken far too often in British industry with disastrous results alike to factory discipline and working pace. Any direct instruction by the personnel manager, production manager, works manager or managing director to workmen undermines the authority of the foremen. It is forgotten far too frequently that it is only by building up the standing and authority of the foremen with the workers under him that a high average of working pace can be achieved.

Where personnel managers, production managers, works managers, and others deal direct with the workers, the authority and standing of the foremen will be low. These are the cases where working pace in a company is likely to be as much as five or ten per cent below the average for the industry or district solely because the authority and standing of the foremen has been lowered in this and other ways.

There are several reasons why this must be the case. The first is the workmen's well known dislike at being forced to take orders or even advice from several persons on the same subject. The second is that it is a common practice for workers in every factory to try to obtain contradictory opinions from different members of the management on the same subject. They do not have to try very hard when several men give them orders or advice. They then use these cases among themselves to prove that the management does not know its own mind. Many managers would be much more guarded in what they say and do, did they know the prevalence of this practice in their own business.

REASONS FOR NATIONAL VARIATIONS

The average foreman and manager, working together as a team may, by good handling of men, raise working pace in a firm to a little above the average of their industry and district. On the other hand they may make mistakes through lack of knowledge which will cost their company quite a considerable sum in loss of output per worker employed, and that without any change in tools or method. There are those who think that the average worker is dull and unintelligent and that university graduates constitute the best brains in the country. That is a matter of opinion. How well the workers work will depend on how well they like the members of the management team, including particularly the foreman and the usual methods of the company. The decision of the workers will be final and not subject to appeal. That is fact. On that decision, unconsciously made, will depend the pace at which they work.

Clearly individual managements, as individuals or as a team, can do nothing to correct slow working pace in a particular industry or in a particular district and bring it up to the level of the best district or industry. Even less are they able to do anything effective to bring the working pace of a nation, where pace is low, up to the level of some other nation. Yet this must obviously be done before British industrial efficiency and prosperity at American levels is possible.

Let us start with the fact that American output per worker on exactly the same work, using the same tools and methods, is considerably higher than in Great Britain. There are exceptions, but in general the rule holds true. It would be easy to give many cases out of my own experience and that of other men to prove that it is true in principle. I believe, however, the fact is too well known to require detailed proof.

That European workers work more slowly when they first arrive is well known in American and Canadian industry. It is the subject of almost universal comment by these workers themselves after they have been a year or two in the country. Most of them express the difference very simply. When they finish a job in Great Britain, they wait for the foreman to tell them what to do next. It is his responsibility; they do not worry about output at all. They work the slow steady gait they have been taught to maintain by their unions and fellow workers. In the United States and Canada they would not wait till they ran out of work to ask the foreman what to do next.

In the United States or Canada in a plant where the relations between workers and management is good, workers appear almost as anxious to maintain output as the foremen. They do not put more effort into their work as a rule than British workers, although they do often work faster and usually more continuously. As the difference has been described to me dozens of times by such men, American workmen use their heads as well as their hands to increase output. They realise that it is output that pays all wages. They boost output as the normal way to secure higher pay.

There is no measurable difference in the capacity of workers of the Northern European nations or of Americans or Canadians to turn out work. About a year or sometimes a little longer in the United States in American industry raises the output of British, French or German workers to American levels. Obviously the man himself has not changed materially in that time. His ideas have. That was all that was necessary.

Logically if British workers held the same ideas as American workers and acted on the same principles, British outputs per worker would be as high as American. The natural question would be what are the ideas that make the difference. By a process of elimination it is possible to show that some ideas do not make any appreciable difference.

American managements have been imported into this country, usually specially selected experienced men. They usually obtain good working pace in British industry, but not better than under the best of British management. Various American incentive schemes have been imported into British industry, but with no great success despite interested parties reporting to the contrary. American methods imported into Britain have been no more successful in improving British working pace than the best of British methods. Clearly the means to improve the national average of British working pace does not lie in any of these.

Questioning workers of European origin in the United States and Canada shows that both the trade unions and the politics of Europe and America are vastly different. Over the years European trade unions have advocated slow working pace and restrictive practices to keep as many men in work as possible in times when jobs were hard to get. That was a normal condition in British industry from 1880 to 1938 except in war-time and in the period immediately following. American trade unions took the opposite view. They boosted output per worker as a means to higher real wages in circumstances where a shortage of labour and rising demand was normal.

Said differently, British trade unions from 1890 onward were far more concerned with the size of their slice of the national cake than they were with the size of the cake for the nation as a whole. They appeared convinced that if the rich got less and they got more, everything in the garden would be lovely. American trade unions worked on the opposite principle. So long as the cake grew steadily larger, and their share of the increase was as large as they thought fair, they were fully satisfied. It is natural that working pace in the two countries, in response to this difference in trade union teaching, was bound also to be very different.

What British workers have demonstrated is that higher incentives in industry will not bribe or induce them to work faster than they think fair. Their solidarity in the circumstances is remarkable. British working pace will not rise to American levels until British trade unions drop their old teachings on working pace and adopt the American view instead. Even then it would take years to accomplish in full. Mistaken habits of work take almost as long to eradicate as mistaken habits of thought.

Differences in working pace between different industries in Great Britain have been affected by several things, the principal one being the degree to which they have suffered shortage of work in the past. Next in importance has been the attitude of trade union leaders in the particular industry and, to a lesser degree, the attitude of the men managing the industry. These are the factors which have the greatest effect on working pace.

Differences in working pace between different areas of the same country cannot be explained away in this way where trade union policy over the country as a whole has been fairly uniform. Differences in working pace that exist between different countries cannot be explained entirely by differences in trade union policy in the countries concerned. This is where politics come in. It would, perhaps, be more correct to say trade union policy and teaching differs more between one country and another when in one country the trade unions had entered politics in full support of one political party and where in the other country the trade unions had kept clear of politics.

A nation is surprisingly like a big company. Men work well if they like the management and think their methods are wise. American trade union leaders and workers believe that theirs is God's country, that the workers get a square deal and that the capitalist system of competitive private enterprise yields them a higher reward than is possible under any other system. They are all set to retain that system and to make it work better. Under these circumstances it is easy to understand that the workers will be satisfied with their system of government and will work well as happy workers usually do.

Exactly the opposite has happened in Great Britain. Acting on political motives, the British trade unions have attacked the capitalist system and have urged the adoption of a new industrial system of their own devising. Instead of making the capitalist system work better, a number of them wish to be able to prove that it cannot be made to work efficiently so that they may be able to enforce its retirement. Again for political reasons they have attacked both the competence and the justice of managements and governments that were not of their way of thinking. They have preached class warfare for many years. In such circumstances it is impossible that British working pace should be as good as American.

57

It has been proven that a British workman works as fast and as effectively as an American worker when his ideas on industry and politics are the same. It is largely a matter of trade union beliefs and aspirations. The British worker absorbs these ideas when he emigrates to the United States. As a result he works well. British workers would work as well as American in this country also, were the same ideas in general use here.

CHAPTER VI

MANAGEMENT IN GENERAL

PRINCIPLES OF GOOD MANAGEMENT

THIS is not a book on management. There is no intention of describing in detail how all the various functions of management should be performed. There are some principles of good management which are or should be common to all techniques of management. Some of these will be described in this chapter which will include some remarks on how managers were chosen in some companies in the past.

In the two following chapters will be described the two sharply opposed techniques of management that are in general use in Great Britain and in other countries. This is necessary to enable the general public, officers and workers to distinguish between the two and to determine which particular technique is used by the firm for which they work. In many cases, however, it will be found that neither system is used in full, but some compromise of the two.

One of these techniques is less costly and more efficient than the others. The operation of both will be analysed to show why this will necessarily be the case. Obviously there are variants of each technique. Why some are more efficient than others will be shown both by analysis and by example.

It is possible to overdo training for some jobs. Many people believe that a fully skilled mechanic will do any mechanical job he may be set better and quicker than a semi-skilled worker. As a young man and as a young manager I held that opinion myself. Practical experience, since repeated on many occasions, proved me wrong.

The first occasion was in Canada. Trade union action had

forced the rates of semi-skilled workmen such as drillers, wheel lathe and axle lathe operators up to the same rates as were paid in the toolroom. We had a slack period and were forced to lay off a number of men. I laid off the men who had been formerly semi-skilled operators and put surplus fully skilled craftsmen and toolroom men in their places. I felt I had made a wise move and one that was in the company's best interests.

I was soon undeceived. These fully skilled men did not turn out nearly as much work as the semi-skilled men who had preceded them. I persevered with the attempt, feeling that given time, their output would rise to former levels. It failed to do so by a very considerable margin. I did everything I knew to speed them up and so justify the decision I had made, but to no avail. As I learned then and on several subsequent occasions, there are jobs on which semi-skilled workers will prove better than the most skilled workers obtainable.

From that almost universal experience there have emerged several sayings common among good practical managers. Do not put on any job a man who is much more fully skilled than the job requires. Do not put a man on a job a boy can do as well or even better. Remember a woman is usually quicker with her fingers than a man. If she can do the job sitting down she will often give a better output than a man.

It is obvious that when these less highly skilled persons who are also less highly paid, turn more work out than highly paid workers on the same job, it pays to use them. This principle has been more intensively used in the United States. In Great Britain fully skilled workmen are used to a far greater degree. It is not that the more skilled men such as toolmakers are lazier. It is that the pace of their work must fall in proportion as the precision with which the work must be done rises. Put a production job into the toolroom and it will always cost far too much.

Another old saying common among managers is that the art of management is merely the art of making wise decisions. Like any other really skilled craftsmen they should produce good decisions which should be capable of passing any inspection and they should be turned out quickly and at a relatively low cost. Another saying is—never use a highly paid executive at a higher level to make a decision or to give an order that a junior executive at a lower level could be trained to do just as well and often better. The latter is a fundamental principle that is too often overlooked.

The reasons are obvious. Decisions made by the junior executive will cost less because his rate per hour is lower. A foreman walking around a factory is usually in sight of and familiar in detail with the job and the persons concerned. Provided only that he is kept fully informed on company policy, his decisions are likely to be sounder decisions than if they are referred to higher levels. It is very important in a factory that decisions should be given quickly and that work should not be delayed from this cause. Work will proceed much more smoothly in factories where junior executives have authority to make decisions. Management will cost less and, if well organised and trained on the job, will usually be more efficient.

Just as soon as some matter concerning day to day work in a factory is referred to higher levels, work and decisions are both delayed and both cost more. The man to whom the matter is referred must have the problem described to him in some detail, or he must go to see it, if his decision is to be a wise one. If the decision is referred to still higher levels, the cost of making the decision and the delay will both be greater.

It is an established principle of good management that as many decisions as possible be made at the lowest executive levels. The emphasis is not so much on training managers as it is on training foremen so thoroughly and selecting them so wisely that after a few years of experience as foremen some of them would make competent managers without further training. It is necessary to teach and constantly to emphasise that every decision that is delayed costs more than it ought to do.

It usually delays work. It discourages those who are awaiting a decision knowing that action is necessary. Good management will see to it that decisions are given promptly.

WISE MANAGERIAL TACTICS

A wise and experienced American trained me in my first post as a manager. It was a big factory. He explained to me the importance of prompt decisions if that factory was to be kept running with maximum efficiency.

I demurred. New at the game, a little more time taken to think things over before making a decision appeared much the wiser course. I told him so.

"You will never make a good leader of men on any such methods," he told me. "Whenever men ask you for a decision, there will usually be some job held up awaiting that decision. They like leaders who know their own mind and who make prompt confident decisions. If you are to make a good manager you must be able to make sound decisions promptly. Those under you will not like delays and will come to believe that you lack knowledge or courage or both."

"There is good reason for their point of view. You expect a good workman to turn out a good job and also to do it quickly. You would not allow him to dawdle just because he felt he might make a mistake. You must learn to do the same in the making of decisions which is your principal task."

He laid down other rules for my guidance. Decisions should not be referred to him when I had the authority to make the decision myself and had the necessary knowledge. I was to learn to stand on my own feet and get on with the job. Matters on which I did not have the authority to act, and they were few, were referred to him. So also were matters on which I lacked experience. He did something other men I have worked for did not always do. He explained in detail the reasons for each decision he gave, against the time when I might be making decisions of that sort myself.

62

Wise managements will insist that decisions should be reached as quickly as possible, preferably in sight of the job. Foremen should make these decisions to as great a degree as possible. This will happen only if they are wisely selected, well trained on the job, kept fully informed on company policy relative to their particular work, and in addition are well backed up by their more senior executives.

There are relatively few decisions that a more senior executive remote from the job seated at a desk in an office can make more wisely. The exceptions are where the decision involves more than one department or section of the business. The more senior executive will have knowledge of these other departments the junior cannot have in as great a degree. Sometimes he will have experience in some phase of the work which the junior lacks. In all such cases the matter should be referred to him. In all other cases under good practical management the junior executive will be told to get on with the job and make his own decisions.

SELECTING MANAGERS

Thirty years ago, ideas as to the kind of men best suited to manage the larger British companies were very different from those held today. Yet even in those early days, views differed widely. Some companies held that all officers above a given rank should, at any rate, be gentlemen. They argued that if the management of a company were to pull together as a team and do good work, they must be congenial to each other by bonds of upbringing, education and early training. Only on that basis would they be able to work together in friendly social equality during office hours and afterwards.

Newly arrived from Canada in 1920 these rules were something of a shock to me. I had been engaged by a large British company as works manager. Prior to my appointment I had been questioned carefully, among other things, about my schooling, and particularly the schools I had attended. No

Canadian could be expected to achieve top marks in such a test, but obviously I did pass. Having done so, at a later date the company's unwritten rules on the subject of qualifications for management were explained to me.

Assuming that their other qualifications were entirely satisfactory, their method of selecting men for the higher posts was simple in the extreme. To be considered at all, the candidate must have been to one of the better known English public schools. That would ensure that he came from the right sort of family; he would not have been taken into the school otherwise. It would ensure that his training at home and at school would have been on similar lines. His manners would be up to the same standard as his education. This was the well known story of the old school tie and all that. On this occasion, however, it was not told as a music hall joke.

The point of view intrigued me. I asked questions. Would a good university degree satisfy them? If in addition the man had been to a suitable public school, the answer was yes; if he had not, the answer was no, definitely. Questioned further they explained why. Some men with the least desirable of manners, personal habits and outlook on life manage to work their way through some universities. Scholastic attainments are all that matter in most universities; bad manners and a crude outlook on life are not deemed sufficiently important to be corrected. The worst of manners, weak morals and a character deficient in many respects will not cause the loss of a mark. There are no honours given at British universities for the highest qualifications in character and manners. These things have ceased to have value except in some public schools.

Canadians have always had a high regard for English politeness and good manners. These they have recognised in the past as being generally superior to their own. Canadians found that it was not the well-to-do in Great Britain who were necessarily the most courteous and polite to strangers. There was a deference and consideration for others shown by persons of the very lowest ranks to the highest, particularly in the countryside, which the younger countries have conspicuously lacked. It is regrettable that manners in Britain are not what they were thirty or forty years ago.

When I was a young man, all the many foremen under whom I served at various times had been promoted from the ranks. This was general throughout American and Canadian industry at that time. Usually superintendents and men of similar rank had previously been foremen. Most of the managers had started on the shop floor, and had had experience in every grade in between. This was then considered by far the best training a manager could have.

An ambitious young man who had served his apprenticeship with a good firm felt he had the best foundation for a successful business career that could be obtained. If he wished to make his ultimate success more certain, he studied at a night school or technical college. He read extensively to get any additional knowledge which he felt he required or which might be useful in his work.

Yet even in those old days, many men in American industry had won university degrees. Managements in those days promoted the best man they could find when they had a higher post to fill. The emphasis was far more on the quality of the individual than on the particular kind of training he might have had. If he had the knowledge and experience necessary to fit him for the job, that was sufficient. It was the best man, and not the man with the best training, who ultimately got the job.

In British industry, the conditions were much the same fifty or more years ago. As a rule the men at the top of the big companies were practical men who won their way up on merit. It is worthy of remark that at the time when British industry led the world, there were practical men in charge almost everywhere. An able and ambitious young man in many of the larger American companies today has little or no chance of promotion unless he has a university degree.

This is a new and particularly American version of the British old school tie idea with university substituted for school. Unfortunately some of the larger British companies are showing signs of taking the same line.

TRAINING MANAGERS

Considerable evidence would be put forward by some persons to prove that men who had worked their way up from the bottom to the top, unaided by influence or a university degree, must necessarily be the best men, and therefore make the best managers. An equally convincing case can be made to show that only a man with a scientific education obtained in a university could ever manage large modern complex companies with maximum efficiency. That the greatest men are those who have won their way up from the bottom to the top without influence, by merit alone, can be established by many examples from modern business, and also from ancient and modern history. That the best leaders and the greatest men have been those born in the purple can be proven as convincingly by the same means. Pre-ordained to leadership, the sons of the great and the wealthy were trained from infancy for the position they would ultimately occupy; no other training for management could possibly be as effective.

What does all this prove? If it be the aim of a company or a country to promote the best, and only the best, then those that have the spark of genius or greatness within them must not be excluded by the accident of birth, education, or even by the kind of business training they were given. If leadership is to go to the most capable, there is no group that can claim that all the ablest are to be found within its ranks. There is no group that can prove that its methods and training are the only ones capable of qualifying men for the higher posts.

The best businesses are usually those which draw their managers both from the practical side and the universities. The country and the businesses of the nation require both.

66

There is something to learn from each. Each learns from the other. Wise managers will see that undue preference is not given to men with either kind of training. It is much more important to discern real ability and the spark of latent leadership in the individual, and to promote only those whose character and ability are worth the training which higher executive authority and experience alone can give. If the right man is chosen and is given his chance, he will not find his past training (or lack of it) much of a handicap. There is an old saying that you cannot keep a good man down.

Business men in the United States today are sending their sons to the universities in ever greater numbers. The reason they do so is plain. It is not because the university has been proven to give better training for management than could be obtained within industry with the assistance of the technical colleges. It is because men holding top management jobs in a number of the larger companies, graduates themselves, have rules that promotions to top jobs should go to men with a like education. In such circumstances, men able to send their sons to universities would be fools if they did not do so, regardless of which type of training was best. Intolerance has done a great deal of harm in industry in the past, and seems destined to continue to do so in the future. The men who introduced the old school tie idea into British industry were at least honest. They did not say that the old school tie made a man a better man, but simply that he was a more pleasant companion.

It has been said that there is very strong propaganda in the United States in favour of university trained men for the top management jobs. The most important, and certainly the highest post in American industry today (1951) is that of industrial mobiliser for the rearmament programme. President Truman chose Mr. Charles E. Wilson for the post. He is not a university trained man. He left school at 13 and won his way to the top of his company the hard way—on merit. Not because he was a practical man, but solely because he was considered the best available man, he was appointed to head the nation's industrial effort. That is as it ought to be in a democracy.

EXPENSIVE MANAGEMENT

In buying clothes, jewellery and similar things a high price is often taken as evidence of a very superior article. This is not true of management. Management is often much more expensive and far less efficient than it ought to be simply because there is far too much of it. Extravagance in management often arises from the use of too many figures, statistics and experts. The most efficient managements I have seen were frugal in the use of staff and figures.

Extravagance in management, as one might expect, is usually most often found in the largest and the wealthiest of companies. This is to be expected. They can afford it. If the management of a very large and profitable company do themselves proud in the way of offices, staff and statistics, there is not likely to be any complaint from the board, provided the profits earned are high enough.

If you wished to find the most extravagant and elaborate management in Great Britain or in the United States, all you need to do is to get a list of the largest and wealthiest companies. Most of them will be found there. A few medium sized companies that have been very profitable over a long period of years may be found in the same category. It is not great size alone, but the combination of great size and great wealth that produces the greatest extravagance in management. The unfortunate thing about it is that these are the companies whose methods of management are so often copied. The general public and many business men do not realise that many of them are very profitable and efficient, not because of their extravagant management, but in spite of it.

One of the commonest mistakes made by individuals and groups visiting the United States is the assumption that the

68

methods of management used by the largest and wealthiest of American companies are necessarily the most efficient. In many cases, the opposite is true. You will find among such companies the most centralised and expensive management and the most elaborate form of accounting and statistics to be found anywhere in the United States. On the other hand there are among these wealthy firms, some where management and accounting is frugal and efficient as it ought to be. The trouble is that many persons visiting the United States, who ought to know better, do not distinguish between these two.

If you know where to look, you can find businesses in the United States which are as frugal and efficiently managed as any in the world. Yet American management varies as widely between extravagance and frugality as management in any other country. American management, however, regardless of whether it is frugal or extravagent, will usually be efficient. Competition compels efficiency and determines the overall level of efficiency which must be attained in order to survive.

CHAPTER VII

PRACTICAL MANAGEMENT

ORIGIN AND DEVELOPMENT

IT is impossible to say when good practical management was first used. It is older than history. It began when one man bossed others to create order out of chaos, to prevent duplication of effort and to get work done with more method and less fatigue. Good practical management could not be described as an exact science, even today. It varies enormously between one business and another and also between one man and the next. There is wisdom in these variations.

There was a time when I was a young man and had achieved some distinction as a manager, that I believed that management was, or ought to be, an exact science, and that I knew in detail which methods were best. That was many years ago. I have learned a great deal since then. Now I know that the best of practical management is not a fixed and arbitrary method. It should be tailored to fit the man who uses it and the business he runs.

When I am asked by some manager, what particular method of practical management he should use, I usually offer him several alternatives, explaining the relative advantages and disadvantages of each. Even under pressure I decline to say which is best, but tell him to select and use the particular variation he prefers, having regard to his own personal preferences, the character of the business and the capacity and training of the men under him. It is my experience that a man is likely to do best on the methods of management he prefers, provided always that the methods from which he makes his selection are all of them sound.

Practical management, as the name implies, covers various techniques of management that have been developed in actual service by practical men. Good practical management is a survival of the fittest of these methods. Having regard to the local conditions, each manager used the methods he thought best. Some methods proved better in use than others. Over the years improvements and refinements were made. If the best of these methods are selected and used, practical management will prove better than any other, not in the class room perhaps, but on the job.

From the commencement, good practical management has always been frugal in the use of figures and of non productive staff generally. It is the technique of management that is almost universal in small businesses and often in medium sized ones as well. The best of practical management carries everything necessary to achieve the maximum of efficiency in operation, but no surpluses.

Good practical management was evolved by trial and error over a long period of time. Practical men have been prepared to try any new and apparently sound theory once, and to make the final decision on the results actually achieved. They use scientists on the class of work for which they are specially trained just as they use draughtsmen, designers and skilled mechanics in work for which particularly skilled and well trained men are necessary. Management was not regarded as a standardized product which could be taught with maximum efficiency in some university or technical college. On the contrary it was regarded as something that was not standard and that only practical experience could shape so as to give the best possible results in a particular business.

Good practical management is management to which the principles of time and motion study have been applied. From the work of the man at the top to the most junior executives all have been under review in an effort to simplify, to reduce costs and to speed decisions. Accounting, statistics, office staff and supervision have been cut down to the lowest level consistent with fully maintained efficiency in operation. Only the observed comparison of the experiences of a number of firms can determine how low it is safe to go without any loss of efficiency.

Practical management at its leanest and most efficient best will not be as popular with some managers as some other techniques, particularly if the company is large and earning a large profit. Among workmen on piecework the parallel would be workers voluntarily suggesting that their piecework prices should be cut because they were too high. There are managers who would be prepared to cut management costs if it could be proven to them that other companies achieved better results for less money. They are not a large percentage of the total but they are the nation's best. They set the pace for the rest.

MANAGEMENT IN LARGE COMPANIES

Good, practical management was developed and perfected in small and medium sized companies. When it was used in large companies the same technique was retained unchanged. In effect each unit of the large company was managed independently as if it were still a separate entity, but owned by the same shareholders as the other units of the same concern. There was very little of central headquarters and very little interference from above in the day to day conduct of affairs by the managers of the decentralized factories or subsidiary businesses.

The principle on which good practical management usually operates in a very large business is that the man or men at the top confine themselves almost entirely to matters of policy. They relinquish detailed control over design, production and sales. Each separate plant is judged on its ability to make a profit and to expand its business. Over the years the junior managers who do well are suitably rewarded. The others are replaced.

There are good sound reasons for this technique. As soon as the top management in any very large company tries to direct production or to control costs in detail, the numbers of top management and the numbers of their technical and office staffs rise sharply. This entails in all cases an even greater rise in the technical and office staffs of the managers next in rank below. The latter increase is usually from two to three times as great as the increase in the ranks of top management and their staffs. Unfortunately the increases do not end there. Staff has to be put on in the factory to get the information required and to carry out instructions passed on from above.

Practical management avoids as far as possible the use of specialized staff in managerial positions. Specialists are used where necessary, but preferably actually on the job and not in managerial posts. The men in charge of time and motion study, production planning, rate setting, tool designing or layout work would be experts at their particular job. These would all come under the foremen, superintendents or ordinary line management as the case might be. Specialized functions of various sorts necessary to the business are things every good practical manager is expected to understand sufficiently well to direct competently.

Good practical managers do not favour the creation of separate sections or departments to deal with some function of management. They may put managers in charge of some section of the work with specialists under them, but these specialists and expert technicians do not manage. This is termed line management. Where specialists in some function of management are allowed to manage other specialists of a similar sort, that particular technique is termed functional management. With rare exceptions good practical management uses line management only. Functional management in any form is obviously much more expensive. Experience shows that the results achieved are not as good as under well organised and well run line management.

MANAGEMENT METHODS COMPARED

In the years just prior to 1914, American industrial consultants were coming into prominence. The two most famous of them, H. L. Gantt and F. W. Taylor taught techniques that were different in principle and in detail. Scientific management, a technique which F. W. Taylor popularised, was winning popularity slowly with managers of some of the larger American companies. In fact I had gone in for it myself to a considerable degree.

The factory I was managing employed some 5,000 men. In my office were a series of record cabinets which I could reach without getting out of my American type revolving office armchair. There were certainly at least fifty different reports and returns covering the work of that factory in considerable detail that were within reach of my hand. I used them daily. Checking them over and taking action on them by letter, by telephone or by having the individuals concerned up to my office constituted a very large portion of my day's work.

About this time I received a visit from the president of a very large and famous American firm which he had founded. After a walk around the factory with this distinguished visitor, I showed him these records and explained the methods by which I attempted to manage the plant. He was not favourably impressed.

"There are two ways of trying to find out what is happening in a large factory," he said. "One is to rely on reports or returns. The other is to go and see for yourself. How many hours a day do you average at this desk and how many do you spend out in the plant?"

I told him an hour to an hour and a half in the factory and the rest of the time at my desk.

"Do you draw your salary mainly as an office man or as an engineer with unusual knowledge of production methods and factory organization," he asked?

I told him the latter. He then told me I should give the

firm who employed me a square deal. A good chief clerk should be able to do most of what I was doing at my desk more quickly and efficiently than I was able to do. "Cut those returns to a third or a half of what you use now. See your seniors on the job in the factory instead of calling them away from their work up to your office. Try to spend most of your day in the factory and as few hours as possible in the office. If you manage to do this successfully I believe you will achieve outstanding success at your work."

It was a great blow to my pride. Nevertheless I took and acted on the advice from that day onward. It was the turning point of my business career. I stopped trying to manage a large factory from a desk in an office. I went back to the sound methods of practical management which my father and the other practical men under whom I had worked had taught me.

Mr. H. L. Gantt completed my conversion. The autocrats at the head of some of the larger American businesses had gone in for scientific management on F. W. Taylor lines in a big way. They and their big staffs of technicians and statisticians ruled these big enterprises in detail from the top. Sitting at a desk in their office they attempted to plan and control in detail production and costs. This they regarded as being the last word in managerial methods.

Gantt took a different view. The general, his staff and the band led the troops only on parade. They went into battle the other way about. The ordinary fighting men and junior officers were up in front attacking the enemy. All the special services were in close support. The success of an operation often depended on how good was the support given to the men who were doing the actual fighting.

Gantt criticised the "parade" attitude of mind on the part of the managers of a business. It was the productive workers only who turned out the work that earned the profit. The foremen should be regarded as being in close support, helping the workers and saving them time and effort to as great a degree as possible. In turn it was the job of management to help the foremen in every way. The importance of this reversed attitude of mind in achieving greater output is not sufficiently well understood, even today.

For a year I had the good fortune to work under this man who was easily the most famous of American consultants in his day. He was insistent on doing away with unnecessary statistics and in delegating authority to lower levels. He emphasised the fewer the figures that were used in a business, the more wisely selected must be the figures that remain. He emphasised the need for good overall control and an absence of unnecessary detail. The Gantt charts were created for that purpose and are very effective in providing an overall control in a very simple form.

The Working End of Management

The best of practical management always regards the foremen as the working end of management, the part that gets the work done. A former member of the T.U.C. gave the same opinion. "No matter what fellows like you think, Ord, working men regard foremen as the management," he said. He then went on to explain the harm that was done on joint consultative committees, works councils and similar bodies when senior members of the management dealt direct with the workers' representatives without the interested foremen being present. He emphasised that information should reach the workers as far as possible through the foremen. It was wise in his opinion to build up the prestige of the foremen and to maintain them in the position of being the effective voice of the management to the workers.

I then told him that I agreed with him fully in all he had said on this point. That is always the policy of the most successful of practical managements. There are other techniques of management which I do not like or recommend which frequently result in the tactical errors of which he complained.

It would be possible to infer that good practical management as I have described it was some precise, clearly defined method of managing a small, medium sized or large business. That is what it is not. Some forty years ago as a young man under the influence of H. L. Gantt I started checking up on the number of non producers various companies in the United States and Canada required to manage and service each hundred persons engaged on actual productive work. A very considerable number of firms were checked over by me in this way.

Some very interesting points emerged at once. The lowest non productive ratio, almost without exception, was where there were good practical men in charge who knew the business thoroughly. Where in a business of any given size, a man managed the business by means of figures and returns from a desk in an office, the non productive ratios were always higher, and sometimes very much higher. It is obvious why this must be so. More detailed information on this subject is available in an earlier book, *Industrial Facts and Fallacies*.

Being a production man myself, I was particularly anxious to discover under which type of management production was most efficient. An honest answer is that it was best sometimes under one method and sometimes under the other. Yet if all the cases I have investigated in the course of my business career be included, the average production was best under the leaner, more practical management. The underlying cause was that production men usually get better support and a clearer understanding of their problems from good experienced practical managements.

There may be some means some day whereby a man sitting at a desk may have some device by which he cannot merely speak to men in the factory, but see the job discussed as clearly as if he was on the spot. That time has not arrived yet. Figures and returns give a cloudy picture at the best. If the men concerned are well selected and well trained, decisions made on the job will, in the great majority of cases, be better and cheaper on average than decisions made by means of returns from a desk in an office. That is what years of investigation on both sides of the Atlantic have taught me.

Reference has been made to the best of practical management. This does not refer to a technique of practical management refined by selection to a definite technique. Were the different firms in some industry in Great Britain or the United States to be investigated on the basis of computation I use, it would be found that some of these firms would have lower non productive ratios than others. Most of the firms with the low ratios would be found to be using good practical management. Most of the high ratio firms would be found to be using scientific management. The highest ratios of all would probably be larger firms who used scientific management with functional management in addition. The firms with the lowest ratios, provided there was no loss in operating efficiency, I would call the best examples of good practical management in that industry.

Of necessity the lowest ratios would use good practical management. In no other way could the proportion of non producers used have been got so low without loss of efficiency. Even these best firms from the point of view of managerial technique, would differ considerably from each other. There would not emerge from any such investigation one precise technique which could be written into a textbook or taught in a class room which would be demonstrably better than the rest. After the theorists have finished, a really experienced practical man can usually make small changes to suit the man and the business which will save a bit here and a bit there with fully maintained efficiency. It is the small changes from the relatively standard pattern which make this improvement possible.

My principal occupation for the last thirty years has been demonstrating to British companies how great are the economies that can always be made by dropping the technique of scientific management in favour of practical management.

The further the point at which work is planned, directed and controlled lies from the place where the work is done, and the less the power to make decisions lies with foremen and junior line executives, the larger would be the possible economies.

The closer the planning and the direction of work is taken to the place where the work is done, the greater will be the economies effected by that change. The larger the amount of paper work and staff that can be removed from higher levels without the loss of operating efficiency, the greater the number of office staff it will be possible to do without. It is not possible to achieve the best possible results overnight, as a considerable amount of training is usually necessary, particularly in the lower ranks of the management. Until foremen can be trained to act, think and speak as junior managers ought to do, good practical management cannot be expected to give the best results of which it is capable.

CHAPTER VIII

SCIENTIFIC MANAGEMENT

Its Origin

Between 1890 and 1915 there were formed a number of very large companies in the United States. The men at the top of some of the largest and most prosperous of these companies were men whose names have since become famous in American industrial history. These men regarded theirs as the master mind on which the success of the business depended. Most of them regarded their subordinates as lesser men in intellectual capacity and soundness of judgment.

Few of them liked the technique of good practical management. It delegated far too much authority to junior executives in their opinion. It allowed the latter far too much latitude in the making of their own plans and the carrying of them through, subject only to the general policy of the company. Moreover practical management did not use sufficient paper work or enough of controls to enable the big man at the top to keep as firm a grip of the details of what was going on in the business as he desired to do.

It was not that men at the head of these big companies did not trust the integrity of their subordinates. It was only that they did not trust their judgment. The men at the top wished to do the planning of their businesses themselves, and in as much detail as was practicable. This involved a complete reversal of the basic principles of good, practical management.

What they wanted was a business run on entirely different principles. They wished to do the planning at headquarters and to pass down instructions in accordance with those plans. They must have sufficient information at headquarters before sound, intelligent plans could be made. It required accurate information as to the progress made in the various plants so that plans could be modified when necessary or steps taken to rectify an altered situation. The instructions passed down to the various factories or agencies must be sufficiently detailed to ensure that these knew exactly what was expected of them. In addition the top management wanted detailed costing to enable a close check to be made on the cost of work done. Scientific management on F. W. Taylor lines was the result.

This type of management was designed, to order, for men who wished to plan and rule the destinies of big companies from the top in as great a detail as was possible. It cost more to manage a business in this way. That was inevitable. None of these men boggled at the price. It gave them what they wanted.

Some of the men at the head of these very large American companies were financial men or speculators. Others were wealthy men who had purchased control of the company, either with their own money or with the assistance of others. Very few of them had a sufficiently long and thorough training in business and industry to be able to run these very large businesses on the methods of good, practical management. As a rule they also lacked the well trained junior staff which is necessary on that technique of management if the business is to be run cheaply and successfully. Scientific management did not require the men at the top to have had any previous experience in industry. That was its great advantage from their point of view.

The reason these men were able to do so well using scientific management in spite of their lack of adequate business training was really very simple. They had a hand picked lot of technical experts to assist them, that a well trained practical manager would not have required. These experts were usually a very capable lot, and were able to do all the headquarters planning that was necessary. Their combined knowledge usually covered every technical and other aspect of the business on which questions were likely to be asked, either by the man at the top or by his subordinates. This technical staff made the plans, watched progress, and reported any variations from schedule with the reasons. From the point of view of men without business training or experience, this was the best technique of management with which they could have been supplied.

The technique of scientific management has another advantage for the man at the top. Such a man, if he is inexperienced, is apt to be asked very awkward questions by experienced managers under him. They are apt to object to plans or suggestions which he puts forward. In any such cases the group of technical assistants gives him all the protection he needs. They answer all the awkward questions. They justify the plans and show that they are possible of accomplishment. They give the man at the top a sense of security that he could not obtain in any other way.

The advantages of scientific management are equally apparent from the point of view of the man or men at the top when it comes to the nationalised industries, where it has been used almost universally. This particular technique enables the government of the day to put in charge of these industries any man they choose, whether he has previous experience in the management of large units or not. This type of management has been installed more completely on what are considered up-to-date lines in the National Coal Board than anywhere else. This was possible largely because the top management organisation was entirely new, and there was nothing old to displace.

By some strange coincidence it is the advocates of scientific management who lay more stress on the need of training for management than anyone else. Obviously this is a strange claim to make, and one that cannot be supported in view of the information given here. It is stranger still in view of some of the nominations that have been made to the higher posts in the nationalised industries.

What was the previous experience in industry, the standard education, and the degree of advanced training for management that the government insisted upon before making nominations to senior posts in the various nationalised industries? These nominations were as mixed a lot in all these particulars as could well have been selected. Who did best? It would be hard to say. It is public knowledge that those who came off worst, in the case of the National Coal Board, were those who knew most about coal.

This agitation for better training for the men at the top of big companies using scientific management comes mainly from persons with training for management to sell. In the front of this movement are university professors, educationalists generally, and industrial consultants. All of them have profited greatly by this drive. They are anxious that it should be intensified. The press, not realising that there is another side to the picture, usually have supported their campaign.

The advantage of scientific management from the point of view of the educationalists, is that it increases the number and the rate of reward of the men who perform the many and varied duties of management, particularly top management. It is natural that they should desire that as many university graduates as possible should secure posts in industry—particularly the higher ones.

The observed results make a farce of their claims that higher education and education for management are essential for success. Men with a minimum of education, with little or no previous experience in industry, and with no special training in management have done quite as well as men with higher education and specialised training, in the management of large businesses and nationalised industries—but only where scientific management with functional management in addition is used. This particular system of management was created to enable untrained men to run the show.

FUNCTIONAL MANAGEMENT

Functional management is not new. It has existed in industry for a hundred years or more. F. W. Taylor, the American industrial consultant, gave the idea new impetus some forty years ago. He urged that only a carpenter foreman should give orders to carpenters—that a foreman in charge of men of each craft must previously have been an experienced craftsman in the particular craft concerned. He urged that the same rule should be applied to all trades and skilled occupations. He recommended that this apply not only to blacksmiths, carpenters, moulders and so on, but also to inspectors, rate setters, production planning, office staffs and so on.

A few persons tried this idea out enthusiastically when it was first suggested. They did not foresee the mess in which it was bound to land them. The rise in the number of foremen required to control a factory of given size, particularly if a wide number of trades was involved, was immense. One foreman might have one craftsman under him, and the next foreman twenty-five or more. This put supervision completely out of balance and made it top heavy.

This new development of the functional management technique had other grave disadvantages. It divided each factory or business into too many small watertight compartments. The cost of management rose sharply. Authority was too heavily subdivided. There were disputes between rival authorities as to their respective jurisdiction, increased jealousies, and considerable confusion. The idea of functional management applied to foremen was soon abandoned.

On the other hand functional management has usually made its appearance sooner or later in any very large and wealthy company which took up the technique of scientific management. It was a natural and almost inevitable process. As has been described, technical experts were grouped round the big man at the top. At first the experts merely gave him any technical information he required, which the big man

84

incorporated in his letters or instructions. As the amount of work done at headquarters steadily increased, and the top man found he had more work awaiting him than he could handle, he had his technical staff write technical letters for him to sign. The duties of his technical assistants still remained advisory only. They could give orders to no one.

The advantages of having technical experts on their own staff to assist them began to become apparent to managers next in rank below. They began to apply the same general technique in their own offices. The greater the amount of information they were asked for by the man at the top and his technical assistants, the more planning that was done and instructions issued from the top level, the greater the numbers of staff they found they required to carry out these instructions. Whenever scientific management is introduced, there is inevitably a growth of staff at top management levels. The greater the amount of work done at top management levels, the more staff that will be required at all levels of management below.

This development of technical staffs at headquarters, at the levels next below, and in very large companies at levels below that again, was what later made functional management almost inevitable. The technical experts at the top level began by giving the big men at the top technical advice. They followed this up by writing his technical letters or letters of instructions for him to sign, sending a copy of this letter as an act of courtesy to the technical expert of like sort in the rank next below. This was not an instruction. It was merely an act of courtesy to keep the more junior technical expert in the same line of work informed on what was going on.

In the course of time the big man at the top in a business using scientific management with functional management in addition, became swamped with the number of letters he had to sign. The next step was for his technical experts to sign letters for him addressed to the manager or managers in the level or levels below. In time such experts usually claim the right to write letters and give orders on their particular subject to the technical man who advises the manager next in rank below on the same subject. Sooner or later they have their way. Management is then split from top to bottom into specialist functions. This development is termed functional management.

There must be divisions of managerial authority and overlapping wherever functional management exists. This occurs, not only at the top, but in all levels below. Jealousies as to authority and jurisdiction break out between "functional managers", as the experts are now called, and the "line managers" who formerly managed the business without any of these new limitations on their authority. Each group strives to extend its authority and enhance its prestige at the expense of others. Rank and file are often in the unfortunate position of having to take orders from both groups. When orders conflict, as is not infrequently the case, confusion and hard feelings result.

It is obvious that the top management and headquarters staff required by a large company using scientific management with functional management in addition must be very much larger than would be required were the same company using good practical management with well trained senior and junior officers. The amount of additional staff will depend upon the size of the company and upon many other factors. It is not intended to go into great detail here to explain how large would be the increase or to give in detail information as to where and why these increases would occur. That should be reserved for a technical book.

GREED FOR POWER

Greed for power on the part of the men at the top of large and medium sized businesses has hampered industrial progress in all countries. This greed manifests itself in a reluctance to delegate authority. The basic principle of good practical management is to delegate as much authority as possible to the lowest practicable level. Scientific management was created for men who refused to delegate authority and who were determined to plan and control large businesses from the top in as great detail as they could contrive.

Ever since men began to manage other men there have occurred times when wise men delegated authority. One such case occurs whenever the number of persons reporting to or under the direct instructions of a particular man passes a certain figure. In some circumstances a foreman may be able to handle as many as twenty-five or even fifty men efficiently without any delegation of authority. The number of persons a man in a more senior position can afford to have reporting to him directly is much smaller. In managerial positions the number might be as few as six or eight. Men who have to spend considerable time dealing directly with the public or with outside firms usually have less time available to spend with the men reporting directly to them. In such cases it is often wise to limit the number of persons reporting to such a man preferably to four or at the most to six.

Able, energetic and ambitious men have always delegated authority with reluctance. The telephone, the teleprinter and the typewriter have enabled a man to supervise much more of business affairs than was possible fifty years ago. A man can and does deal with many more important matters without leaving his desk than was possible a hundred years ago. There is an opposite side to this situation. Many senior executives today deal with more detail than is wise or necessary. In such cases men would be wise if they delegated some of the detail to junior executives and left themselves more time for the consideration of more important matters.

Every senior executive has, on several occasions in his career, the important problem to consider of what to do himself and what to delegate to others. It is always a difficult decision to make. It will usually be determined largely by his early training in industry. It will also be affected by the character of the men under him and the degree to which he trusts them. Upon this decision will depend in large measure the cost and efficiency of management in the firm concerned.

It is a rule of good practical management that the men at the top should not have a deputy. The habit of having joint managing directors, for example is against the principles of good management. When the man at the top, or any other person, has too much work to do he should delegate some of his duties to lower levels. There is no use saying that this cannot be done. It is done universally in the largest and most efficient of American companies. It can be done in others if the will to do it is there.

The object of appointing joint managing directors, for example, or of appointing deputies to the men at the top, is merely the creation of more senior well paid posts. These posts may be created as a reward for good service or to provide a job near the top for persons so influential that their claims could not be overlooked. Under good practical management appointments of this sort would not be necessary and would not be made. One of the attractions of scientific management in the eyes of some people is the large number of senior posts it finds excuses to create.

The appointment of deputies to the men in the top jobs is almost universal in the nationalised British industries. This is understandable. The same thing occurs in most of the larger privately owned companies that use scientific management with functional management in addition. These latter companies also have the habit of appointing personal assistants to the men at the top or to men in other senior posts. The reason given is that the man at the top is too busy and therefore requires help of this sort. That is not the case. The man concerned is attempting to do too much. In spite of being overloaded, he will not delegate authority. A personal assistant is not the wisest move to cure such a situation.

Personal assistants are used occasionally in American industry. Usually these assistants are unpopular because of the unfortunate situation they create. They can achieve power in the organisation only in proportion as some regular line manager in the level next below is forced to relinquish it. To any informed observer the appointment of a personal assistant is merely another attempt by the man at the top to grasp and to hold more power than he ought to be permitted to do, or to advance some personal supporter to a position of greater power.

There is a danger in making appointments of this sort. A wise American industrialist remarked to me that few men at the top of big businesses were unpopular because of things they themselves had said or done. Much is forgiven of the man at the top, particularly if he is able and successful. Damage to his reputation or popularity within the firm is usually done by those who speak in his name. Personal assistants are hostages to fortune in this particular. Under good, practical management they would not be used. Managers at lower levels would be given their chance in the form of more work, and authority delegated to them.

BEST BRAINS FOR TOP POSTS

There is no subject on which opinions differ more widely than on the availability of bright intellects in the lower ranks of industry. Men who have won their way from the bottom to the top of a big business on merit, usually say that there are plenty of men fit for promotion to management to be found in the lower ranks of their own businesses. They give apprentices a particularly thorough training. They pick the best of them and go to considerable trouble to train them to make good foremen. The best of the foremen are trained to become superintendents or works managers. Some reach still higher posts. This is normal under good, practical management.

Men who have won their way to the top from the lower ranks appreciate the importance of selecting and training the future officers of the firm in the same way they were trained.

They realise the importance of the foremen as the normal point of contact with the workers. They realise that the foremen supervise all the productive work done within the plant and constitute the working end of management. Top management theorises and talks. The bottom end starts the work and sees it through to a finish.

A principal reason practical managers are not keen on university trained men in industry is that the universities do not attempt to turn out well trained foremen. Either universities do not consider it a worthwhile task, or alternatively they recognise it as something that they are not able to do as well as is necessary. They have given up the attempt and have concentrated on management. The final result is absurd. The universities cannot train foremen and claim to be able to turn out competent managers. Imagine the Royal Navy setting up a naval college that would take in raw recruits and turn out fully trained admirals without being able to turn out officers of lower rank!

Practical managers who have won their way from the bottom to the top on merit do not like university training for management for another reason. Men who have won their way up from bottom to top on merit have been convinced by their own experience that promotion stage by stage from the bottom to the top such as they had, and is normal in the navy or the army, is the best method. Moreover the universities usually train all their graduates in the principles of scientific management without realising that good, practical management is the better technique and one that is in general use in the majority of the smaller companies and usually in the more efficient of the larger ones. University trained men therefore create a difficulty for businesses which use the technique of good practical management.

CHAPTER IX

RUSSIAN INDUSTRIALISATION

ADVANTAGES OF DICTATORSHIP

THE Russian leaders felt at the time they founded their present system, that one of the disadvantages of a true democracy is that social and industrial progress is often very slow. If government is by the people, and if the will of the people is accurately reflected in the policies and actions of the government, then progress can be made only as fast as the wishes and beliefs of the great majority of the population change and move forward. No matter how much effort may be made to educate people to a new point of view, and no matter how wisely this may be done, it is necessarily a very slow process. Russian leaders believed the industrial progress of the true democracies had been slow and irregular mainly due to the difficulties in training the masses. Had progress been planned on a national scale by a wise state that was also authoritarian, it was their conviction that progress would have been much more rapid. At any rate that was the method they decided to use.

The Russian leaders recognized that theirs was a backward nation socially and industrially. Even more backward was the standard of thinking and education. They believed a dictatorship would enable them to make the necessary moves to raise industrial efficiency and the standard of living of the people more rapidly than was possible in a true democracy.

They did not do what they so easily might have done in such circumstances—work out new industrial and economic theories of their own. They recognised the fact that industrially the United States was in the lead—and by a wide margin. Their representatives visited the United States, inspected American factories and their methods. They made heavy purchases of plant and equipment, manufactured goods and other things in that country. They read American industrial textbooks, employed American advisers, and after a period of intensive study, decided on the industrial procedure and technique they would use.

The United States had, on average, the most efficient industries in the world. The Americans had been in the lead for a long time. Their lead was still increasing. Obviously in such circumstances their methods must be the best—well tried and dependable. The Russians decided they could not do better than copy the American production technique in full and without change, at least to start with.

Even at that, they did not copy blindly. They studied carefully the American textbooks in factory location. They gave careful consideration to the various American designs of factory construction, layout and specialized handling equipment. They studied the best of American books on production planning, material control, time and motion study and similar subjects. A few of the best known of these books were translated into Russian. The more usual procedure was for Russian professors to read these books in the original English and then to write books on the same subjects in Russian. In the main these books adhered closely to the general principles and to much of the detail given in the American text.

If the production side were taken in hand first, the paper side was not neglected. American books on accounting, works and cost accounting, budgetary control and statistics were treated in the same way. American methods of storekeeping, stock records, progressing work and deliveries were described in books written in Russian by Russian authors. These gave in Russian what was in reality up-to-date American practice in these matters.

The Russians were convinced that more university education in particular was essential if their industrial development was to get under way quickly and on a sound basis. Their universities and technical colleges were enlarged to an enormous degree. Production and industrial technology were taught. These generally were on American lines, but with Russian social and political presentation. There can be few jobs of industrial teaching and training that have been done more thoroughly than in Russia.

The Russians were realists, however; they put first things first. They knew that machines with power to drive them formed the basis of the Industrial Revolution. They knew the Americans were in the lead primarily because they had more and better machines with more power to drive them than any other nation. It was their intention to reach American standards or better in the matter of industrial tools and equipment of all sorts. They started with agricultural and followed up with mining, manufacturing and other industrial activities.

The Russian transportation system was inadequate. Moscow today has an excellent system of underground railways. The Russian railway system has been improved, re-equipped and extended. A very remarkable system of canals has been installed. Road making has gone ahead rapidly. Perhaps the most remarkable of the Russian developments has been their huge dams to provide the additional power they require and also to enable them to undertake irrigation of desert lands.

RUSSIAN PRODUCTION METHODS

The Russians considered that it was unwise to try to improve on American production methods, at least until their industries were well established and had time to settle down. The quickest way to get going was to copy American production machines and methods in exact and careful detail. This is what they did in the great majority of cases, even to importing the machines along with the methods.

Their technique in tackling this problem was essentially

93

safe. For example they went to the United States and selected certain makes of motor cars and of trucks which enjoyed a particularly good reputation for reliability and which they considered most suitable for their purpose. In some cases they purchased the entire jig and tool equipment for making a particular model from the makers of the car with all the necessary drawings, blue prints and other instructions. They purchased duplicates of the machine tools used by the motor car manufacturer from the various machine tool makers.

They would pay a considerable sum for permission to make a particular model in Russia. Then they would employ experienced American engineers to go to Russia to supervise the layout of the factories necessary to make the motor cars and other products. These men would also supervise the installation of the machines, jigs and tools and would stay until the factories were in production with the early starting difficulties all ironed out.

Factory after factory was built to make American products, using American machine tools, jigs and handling equipment. These were supervised by American engineers and were used as pilot plants to train Russian industry at all levels in American production methods. These acted as prototypes of the many other factories built and supervised by Russian engineers to make other products without outside assistance. Many of these latter factories are as up-to-date in their equipment and production methods as any in the world.

Not merely have the Russians built factories to make motor cars, tractors, locomotives, textiles, boots and shoes and similar things. They have gone much further. They now make all or almost all the machines, machine tools and other equipment required to make these products and so make Russia self sufficient to as great a degree as possible. In the main they have copied American machines. Where in particular cases they have thought a German, Swiss or British design was best, they have copied them instead. They have always imported into their country, sample machines of new or advanced design to as great a degree as they were able and have copied their best features.

No nation watches the industrial progress of other nations more carefully than Russia. No nation is readier to copy others when she finds they have something better. It would be difficult to suggest sounder tactics than Russia used in developing, expanding and improving her national production. Today they have some of the most modern and up-to-date factories in the world with well trained staff to man them.

The Russians confined themselves to copying the products of other countries, industrial and military, when they first started. It was not long before they were attempting to improve on the imported products. Later they began to bring out their own designs. Some of these have been very good, and in some cases the Russian designed and manufactured products have proved superior to any made by the Western world. The Russians had the best heavy tanks in the last great war. Their M.I.G. jet fighters over Korea are considered by many to be superior to any the United Nations can put in the air against them at this present time. The jet engine with which they are powered is said to be a better engine than the British one from which it was developed. These points are mentioned merely as evidence of how far Russia has travelled industrially since the Soviet Union was formed.

STANDARDIZATION

The Russians were careful to learn all they could from Americans as to the true reasons for the more rapid American industrial advance. Standardization, they were told, was one of the principal reasons. This has been carried much further in America than in Europe or elsewhere. American business men, university professors and books gave clear explanations of the reductions in manufacturing, sales and distribution costs when there is a considerable measure of standardization.

These explained the reasons for the additional manufacturing costs incurred when American motor cars and other products are changed considerably for sales reasons each year. Even in the United States, fashion and sales policy will not allow rigid standardization. These considerations limit the amount of standardization possible in that country.

The Russians decided that there were gains to be made in carrying standardization further than was considered wise or attainable in the United States. Before they put a new product into production, whether it is of a design copied or adapted from some other country or a new design of their own, it is first tested thoroughly. When it finally goes into quantity production, if it is quite satisfactory, it may run five or even ten years without a change. Design changes will be made only to improve the product, to simplify or cheapen production.

There are no competing models of a similar size or kind. Products like motor cars or trucks would get the whole of the available market. Because of this lack of variety and the absence of competition, the total volume of some products made is often greater than in the United States. The output is much more even from month to month. There is no doubt that Russian industry, from a production point of view, often enjoys considerable advantages over American. The former are free from fashion changes, know the output that will be required of them month after month and year after year with far greater accuracy than is possible in the U.S.A. Russian monthly outputs vary less, a very important point in achieving efficient production.

Another widely held American belief is that the cheapness of their products is determined in a large measure by the size of the factory that produces them. The Russians investigated this belief and came to the conclusion that the volume of a particular product that was made in a single unit or factory did have a considerable effect on the rate and cost of production. They accepted the general American belief that small factories cannot make products that are required in great volume as cheaply as large factories. Because their factories were most of them new, the Russians were able to build their factories to the ideal size having regard to the product and the rate of production required. In this particular they probably hold some advantage over the United States.

American manufacturing facilities sprang up all over the United States and for a variety of reasons. In some lines of business there are far too many manufacturing units for the maximum of manufacturing efficiency. Many of them are badly located both as to their raw material supply and the markets they serve. The availability of suitable labour, of cheap power, the money the firm had to spend and where the proprietors lived were the sort of reasons that determined the number, the size and the location of many American manufacturing units.

Russia determined that her manufacturing units should be built of the ideal size and at strategically the best possible location. The availability of labour did not bother them. They decided on the best site and moved the necessary labour there when that was necessary. These factories were put where, with relation to the supply of raw materials, available power, and the markets they would serve, they would operate most efficiently.

By and large Russia's manufacturing units have been better planned for efficient production and better sited than those of any other country. Only a totalitarian state with a high regard for industrial efficiency and an almost complete disregard for other considerations, except perhaps military ones, could have carried such ideas into practice so completely. Over the last fifteen years or more, dispersal of industry from military necessity has added to their problems. They have been forced to place some plants where they were safest rather than in the best economic position. In spite of this fact it is probable that Russia's manufacturing units are more wisely sited on average than those of the United States.

RUSSIAN METHODS IN MANAGEMENT

The Russians accepted in full the usual American assertions that their industrial leadership was due to better management. Put differently, the American contention was that they led because they had a larger percentage of full time graduates from their universities and technical colleges in managerial positions in industry than any other country. They also believed that the particular technique of management taught in the American universities and technical colleges, usually referred to as scientific management, was superior to the techniques taught in any other country. All these statements the Russians accepted as being true, proved they considered, by the clearly demonstrated average superiority of American industry over the rest of the world.

There was nothing in the American industrial technique that appealed to the men at the head of the Russian government more than scientific management with functional management in addition on true F. W. Taylor lines. It was industrially the same technique as they proposed to apply politically. Direction, planning and controls were firmly in the hands of the few at the top. The two techniques fitted each other exactly. They were complementary. Scientific management was adopted with enthusiasm and complete conviction.

The Russians accepted another popular American belief with equal enthusiasm. Very large corporations (as distinct from large factory units) are believed by most Americans to be one of the fundamental reasons for American industrial leadership. This arises largely from excellent and maintained propaganda by the big companies who get an excellent press, and for obvious reasons. Lists of the largest American companies are published from time to time, giving the volume of business done by each company in the year, the total number of employees, the amount of capital involved, the total profits and any other items of news likely to interest the public. This is usually followed by a write-up emphasising the value to the nation of these very large corporations and stressing the rise in efficiency that follows their increasing size. The Russians accepted these statements as true and determined that their business organisations, if fewer in number, should be even bigger.

They are. The Russians decided if great size made businesses more efficient, that they would have no small ones. All the small units in the country, whether for manufacturing, mining, distribution, belong to some large corporation as great in size as the larger American corporations. It is a fact that the average Russian business organisation is considerably larger than the average in the United States.

In the training of men for management the Russians are out to outdo the United States and every other nation. The men at the head of the Soviet Union recognised that the Russian peasants and workers were an illiterate lot, lacking in industrial skill and knowledge. Accepting the view of many Americans in high positions that their leadership in industry was due mainly to the high percentage of men managing businesses who were full time graduates of universities or technical colleges, the Russians determined to outdo them on this point as well. They enlarged their universities and technical colleges. They built many new ones. They determined that the new appointments to managerial posts should be men with suitable degrees to as great a degree as they could contrive. It is probable that Russia has a percentage of men with a university education holding key positions in industry that compares favourably with the United States.

Education costs money. Higher education costs more. A university education is the most costly of the lot. Russia had no intention of providing a university education to all and sundry on the scale that is practised in the United States. In the Russian view, most of the American university education is wasted. It is given to many persons unable to make efficient use of education to that high standard. The Russians intended to ensure that men get the standard of education that their jobs required. They intended that expensive university education should not be given where it was not required.

The Russians were logical and accepted other features of American economic and industrial teaching in the universities. If these giant Russian corporations which were built up of one or even of several nationalised industries, were to be kept in step with each other and serious surpluses or shortages were to be avoided, it was clear that they must be linked together at the top and their activities co-ordinated. Another term for the sort of organisation they favoured was the "planned economy". It was the sort of scientific planning of a nation's production which had long been advocated by economists in some of the leading American universities and by similar men in other countries.

The final Russian industrial organisation was not on the pattern that exists in the United States. Rather it was the sort of ideal organisation that might have existed had American intellectuals been able to have their way and to plan and run the country on the lines they thought best. If scientific management was the best technique and if very large companies were more efficient than small ones, then the moves the Russians made were sound. The Russians also set up planning boards at cabinet level to draw up their great five year plans for industry and to set the great national corporations their tasks.

In one other respect the technique of management in Russian industry has proven superior to American. Regardless of whether times are good or bad, there is always full employment in Russia. The industries of the nation and its man and woman power are always being used to the maximum limit of their capacity to turn out real wealth for the nation as a whole. It is a challenge to the originality and the far sightedness of the leaders of the democracies who, so far, have been unable to plan and accomplish a similar result as successfully.

It will be apparent from the foregoing that the Russians did not theorise or invent new industrial techniques. No other nation in the world has accepted and acted on the technique of scientific management as taught in the United States to the degree Russia has done—not even the United States herself. Russia has gone far in ensuring that the management of industry shall be performed by men with suitable university degrees. She has carried standardization further than Americans have been able or willing to do. She has relatively fewer small factory units and small businesses than the U.S.A. She has reduced the standard of living of the ordinary folk to a degree the United States would not dare to do in order to provide additional capital equipment for industry more rapidly. If these commonly accepted American industrial beliefs be true, then one day Russia should certainly lead the United States in industrial efficiency and in the production of real wealth per head.

Lessons from the Russian Experiment

Each nation should adopt whatever industrial system is capable of yielding them the highest possible output of real wealth per head and the highest industrial efficiency. An even better test would be that the system used should give the workers of the country concerned either the highest real wages in the world or something very close to that level. That a high output of real wealth for a nation and high real wages for the workers of a country are quite separate matters will be emphasised in a later chapter.

American industrial success is founded on their anti-trust laws. These make the conditions under which American industry operates very different and much more compelling of efficiency than in other countries. Sharp and unrestricted competition is the objective of these laws, the encouragement of small companies and the suppression of large ones. The raising and maintaining of prices by agreement, the allocation of work or territory, and the formation of monopolies or cartels are also forbidden by these laws. The Russians, like the British, have omitted these precautions. They have adopted in their place, central planning by governments and the type of scientific management popular with American intellectuals. In other words Russian industry is organised on exactly the same lines as would occur were all British industry to be nationalised on Socialist lines.

Everyone is interested to know how the Russian experiment worked out. Unfortunately it is impossible to get exact figures of the Russian production of real wealth per head. It is even harder to get an accurate comparison of Russian real wages with British or American. Many estimates have been made. These vary widely. American real wages are believed to be somewhere from three to five times the Russian level. British real wages are said to be from one and a half anywhere up to three times Russian. You can take your choice and select between these extremes the ratio you prefer to believe.

Russian industrialisation has certainly proceeded further than in New Zealand or Australia. It is probably pretty well up to the Canadian standard per head of the population. It is therefore time that Russia began to show worthwhile results.

Real wages in the three Commonwealth countries are pretty nearly up to American levels. They are therefore three or four times as high as Russian. Clearly the Russians have made some very serious mistakes in their attempts to copy and improve upon American industrial performance. They certainly should be doing very much better than they are today, considering the amount of industrialisation that has already taken place.

The industrial mistakes that Russia has made have been repeated in Socialist Britain. The British mistakes are not as serious as the Russian because at present they do not go as far. In both countries the mistakes are those that are inherent and inevitable in any centralised industrial system run or controlled by a central government. These mistakes cannot be eradicated, regardless of whether the government concerned is of the left or the right. When sharp and unrestricted competition finally dies, and the big units planned from the top take its place, with industry operating under plans prepared by the state, the form that industry must then take is pretty clearly defined.

What the Russian experiment clearly proves is that you cannot take American machines, methods and production technique, transplant them to some other country under totally different industrial conditions, and have them operate as efficiently as in the United States. A great deal of emphasis has been laid here on the importance of various industrial techniques in detail. There is plenty of evidence available to show that they are important. Yet the Russian experiment shows that other things matter more.

There is no doubt that the Russian production methods are good. The Russian effort certainly did not fail in that direction. On the other hand Russian working pace is known to be slower than American; that is one point where the Russians have failed. Another is that the non productive ratios in industry and throughout the country are higher; that is an even more important point where the Russians have failed. What is to be learned from all this?

It is possible for a great nation to copy American production methods, machines and organisation closely and faithfully. Take the American production organisation out from under their system of competitive private enterprise, and try to run the same production machine under a state owned industrial system planned from the top, and the results achieved will be surprisingly poor. That is the lesson to be learned from the Russian experiment.

The world should be grateful to the Russians for trying out more thoroughly than the United States has done the new American theories of state planning, big companies, and scientific management. American production tools and methods are best. Some American theories of governmental planning, higher education and scientific management are far less efficient than the older, more practical methods they replaced. Russian industrial backwardness and in particular the Russian worker's low standard of living today is largely due to the Russian mistake of adopting too fully and completely many mistaken American theories.

CHAPTER X

PRODUCTION TECHNIQUE

PRODUCTIVITY

STATEMENTS are frequently made such as "increasing productivity is the greatest need of the nation today". The word productivity is used in so many different applications by so many persons that its real meaning is clouded. Production and productivity certainly have different meanings today. Production technique will be defined in this chapter.

When the Anglo-American Productivity Council was formed the then British Government insisted that its activities be limited to production problems only. This was a political move which was unfortunate for the nation. It kept the attention of the public and of business men directed too closely at production problems only, and not enough attention was paid to the conditions under which industry in general and production in particular was carried on in Great Britain and the United States.

One important point must not be overlooked. It has been shown that American production men and American firms in Great Britain do little if any better than their leading British competitors. This would indicate that American management technique is not as far ahead of British as the British public have been led to believe. This is confirmed by the fact that British firms in the United States, often under British managers, do quite as well as their American competitors.

Americans who are asked to explain this strange situation usually evade a direct answer. Many say frankly they do not know the reasons. Yet a correct and detailed answer is necessary before the British people can solve their production and industrial problems and make their businesses as efficient as American.

The explanation is a simple one. In the main British production men are as knowledgeable and capable as American. The latter, however, enjoy industrial advantages which will keep them in the lead of their British opposite numbers for as long as these unequal conditions continue. Some of the conditions which operate to the advantage of American production men will be mentioned in this chapter.

British working pace is slower than American. British trade unions use restrictive practices while American trade unions in the main do not. These two factors constitute a major advantage for the American production man. Unfortunately they are matters which are largely outside the control of production men as was shown in the chapter on "Working Pace and Incentives". How well men work and how effectively they co-operate to increase output is a joint responsibility shared between trade union leaders, politicians and senior business men. Production men do not have a large part in shaping the final result.

The Russian industrial experiment proved that national prosperity and real wages will not necessarily be high even if the production technique of the nation concerned is really good. The conditions under which industry is made to operate have more effect on the final result than production technique. For example, if British production tools and methods could be raised to American levels tomorrow by some miracle, British industrial production per head for the nation as a whole would still remain far below American levels. In fact the amount of improvement that would take place would be disappointingly small. This is one of the most important facts for British business men and the general public to learn.

The statement made above might be put in a different way. How to solve British production problems is only a small part of what it is necessary to learn from the United States. The reason why production men who are no more capable accomplish better results in the United States is because the conditions under which they operate give them material advantages. The reasons American businesses operate at lower levels of efficiency in Great Britain than in the United States proves that the conditions under which businesses operate in this country are not as conducive to efficiency as are the conditions in the United States. It is far more necessary to learn what are these other factors which contribute to American industrial success than it is to learn the details of American production technique.

It would not be intelligent to criticise the kitchen layout and equipment or the furnishings of a poor person's house. It is probable that what they have is all they can reasonably afford. No matter how great their knowledge of what is possible or desirable, what such persons can do is always limited by the amount of money they have available for such purposes.

The same principle holds true in business. It is not intelligent to criticize the man or men directly in charge of production in British plants if their machines and equipment are obsolete. It needs money, and often large sums of money, to install production tools up to American standards in quantity and quality. The money for new tools and equipment is provided in the main, either directly or indirectly, out of profits. Only if profits are high and competition is really sharp and unrestricted will the most up-to-date of plant and equipment be provided. This is the principal advantage which American production men enjoy.

It is wise and factual to assume that production men in all countries will have plant and equipment as modern and up-to-date as they can persuade their directors to buy. Factors which were described above, factors that are quite outside the production man's direct control, determine how up-to-date will be the equipment with which he is furnished. It is not a matter of what he knows. All production men are keen to learn. The eagerness of the British production teams to pick out and use the best points of American production technique prove that. To obtain the best possible production equipment, not knowledge but money is wanted.

American production men enjoy other advantages. American firms encourage their production men to become members of various technical associations. They are given leave and are expected to travel to meetings which are held away from their home town and are told to do this at the firm's expense. In many cases their membership fees are paid. More important, production men are encouraged to visit firms in the same or in other lines of business as frequently as they can conveniently arrange. This is usual in American industry where exchange visits between firms are commonplace. In addition there is very free exchange of information on production problems between firms in the same or in different industries.

It is not only on money spent on new machines and handling equipment that the American production man enjoys a great advantage. He is also given very much more money to spend on jigs and fixtures and on trying out new methods of production. In fact if anything comes along that appears to promise better results, American production men are given a much freer hand in trying them out, even if changes in design of the product would be necessary to make the maximum economies possible. Undoubtedly these things all go to make the American production man's task easier than it is for the average production man in British firms.

British Production Men

The extent of a man's production knowledge is usually determined by the total of his production experience. It is determined even more by the degree to which he is moved about from business to business to see how other firms solve production problems. This is knowledge which cannot be found in any book. It cannot be taught in any university. To make a man a leading production man in a particular industry requires many years of travel and study, several times as long as would be required to obtain a degree in a university. It would require mechanical equipment and a volume and variety of production that no university possesses. In fact university professors who wish to teach production technique in a realistic way must first go out into industry to acquire the knowledge they would need for that purpose.

A thorough production training in industry cannot be obtained with one firm, if the firm concerned happens to be a small one. This point cannot be emphasised too strongly. If the production man of a small firm is to be thoroughly trained, this can be accomplished only by giving the man concerned the opportunity of visiting many firms in the same or in other industries.

I received my early training with a very large firm. They operated many factories. I visited all of them and worked in eight, including the largest. My chief, an American, said this training was not broad enough to give me all the knowledge a good production man required. He instructed me to visit one famous American factory each month. This training was continued over a five-year period. The visits did not work out at exactly one each month, but I did visit more than twelve American plants each year for more than five years. This was excellent production training. I commend the method to others.

This occurred more than thirty years ago. I learned so much in this way that I have continued to visit factories whenever the opportunity offered ever since. This is essential if a production man is really to keep his knowledge up-to-date. The more years you spend at it the more you find to learn.

It may not be easy for small firms to give their production men training as wide and as varied as I had. At any rate they should do as much as they can in this direction. In addition all men engaged on production should be furnished with up-to-date trade and technical journals covering their line of business, both British and American. While the United States continues to lead industrially to the degree that it does today, few good American technical journals are essential.

Many firms circulate technical journals only among the senior executives. This is a mistake. They should be circulated down to foreman levels at least. If the company is a large one, several copies of some journals may be necessary. Where one copy only is used it is dilapidated and months old before it reaches the last name on the list.

Any firm that considers itself relatively up-to-date should have a lending library of well selected technical books. A small firm would find fifty or a hundred books of that sort a very worthwhile investment. These books should be made available to apprentices, craftsmen, draughtsmen and office staffs as well as to the more senior personnel.

Throughout this book emphasis has been laid on the fact that every firm, other than the very smallest, is or should be, a training institution. They train apprentices. Some firms do this job thoroughly and ensure that the boys get technical college training as well. Relatively few firms in the past have done planned and organized training above apprentice level. It is very necessary, and particularly on production problems.

Production technique is not static. There is a steady stream of new machine tools, small tools, handling equipment and other mechanical gadgets that are in most cases a considerable improvement on what was available in the past. New materials, methods and processes are constantly being brought out. A man must do a lot of reading to keep up-to-date. Some of these developments that are of considerable interest to a company are often difficult to describe in a short article in a technical magazine.

It would be wise for companies to arrange lectures from time to time to keep staff and workpeople interested in these new developments. Companies responsible for the new developments will usually be willing to supply lecturers who are informed on the subject—usually without charge. On other occasions it will be found that there are persons on the company's staff able to give a good talk on a subject of interest to the company's employees. Activities of this sort should be encouraged provided always that they are and remain popular with the company's staff and workpeople. No pressure should be used to make any of them attend. Obviously it is as important to keep men up-to-date as it was to train them in the first place.

TOOLS FOR PRODUCTION

Some persons believe the reason British tools for production are less up-to-date than American is due to lack of knowledge on the part of British production men. That is absurd. As a rule the latter are fully aware which machine, British or American, would be best for a particular job. They would buy only the best, were they given the necessary money. British production equipment is inferior to American only because the men in charge were not given sufficient money to spend.

It is true that British production men in many businesses are not as well informed on American machine tools and equipment as they were prior to 1939. Fewer American technical magazines, machine tool and speciality catalogues are available than was the case in 1940 or earlier. Dollars are hard to get for the purchase of magazines or machines. It is a pity when anything happens to prevent production men looking for and obtaining whatever equipment is best for their purpose.

It has been said earlier that the efficiency of the machines, tools and methods of production used by the industries of a nation do not depend primarily on the knowledge of their production men. The industrial and political system under which production must operate is the controlling factor. The most up-to-date and efficient of production tools are usually the most expensive. To keep the tools and equipment of a business fully up-to-date in all respects obviously will cost a lot of money. Knowledge of production, no matter how great, cannot be used as a substitute for money to obtain the machines that the possessor of that knowledge knows is required.

A principal advantage of American production men is that they pay double, or more than double, British wage rates. Because of costlier labour, American managements are more willing to spend capital on labour saving machines. Many of the newest and most up-to-date machines are American for this cause alone. Many of these American machines were developed only because of the more expensive American labour. It would not pay to install some of the newest machines in countries where labour is relatively cheap. Because British labour is cheap it often does not pay to design and build similar machines in this country. Because of the greater demand, many American machines of this sort are cheaper to buy than British. While these conditions continue the capital equipment of American industries will be superior to British.

Any business man will realise the advantage this situation gives to American production men. More expensive labour and cheaper machine tools make it easier for him to show the management that a particular machine can be purchased and paid for out of savings over a five year period or whatever other basic calculation the particular company uses. With cheaper labour and relatively more expensive machines, the British production man would be quite unable to make a case for the purchase of the same or a similar machine even though the actual shop conditions were very similar in both cases.

This was one of the first things I learned when I came to this country thirty years ago to install American production methods. The directors of the company concerned soon convinced me that I could not justify financially spending money on machine tools and other capital equipment at the same rate that I would have done in the United States or Canada. Little as I liked it, I found what they said was true. It was not something that any amount of production knowledge could cure. It was something that was controlled by the industrial conditions within each country. These conditions give the American production man a long lead.

That the conditions under which industry and in particular production operates in the two countries are vastly different is something which British politicians, economists and trade union leaders try to evade. They refuse to acknowledge that these conditions have made it inevitable that American capital equipment should be markedly superior to British in the past. Much more serious, they refuse to see that while these conditions continue the American lead in more and more up-to-date tools for industry must inevitably grow greater in the future.

For any business in any country to have the best of tools and equipment, the directing heads of the business must be able to raise or provide the money and be willing to spend it for this purpose. In a democratic country operating on the capitalist system, ample profits are necessary. Experience proves that sharp and unrestricted competition is equally necessary. A good production man is in the strongest position where the profits are good, and as a consequence plenty of money is available. On the other hand really sharp competition and the relative certainty that if his plant and equipment is not of the best he will not be able to make a profit at all puts him in the strongest position to get what he requires. The combination of these two factors explains the reasons for American leadership in capital tools for industry.

Many American firms install new machines and better equipment only because they must if they are to survive the sharp competition they have to meet. Were competition less keen in their particular industry, the machines would not have been installed. There are many such cases. These are proven facts.

In complete contrast was the situation in one large British company of which I was managing director. We had one very large factory not fifteen years old. Technical progress in that industry had made it relatively out of date. Re-equipment on the most modern lines would have been very costly. The new equipment would double output capacity and reduce costs sharply.

We belonged to a trade association which I approached to discuss the situation. They would not agree either to our reducing our selling prices or to increase our allocation. We would be fined if we took more than our percentage of the total trade. Informally we argued about the matter. The right thing to do they said was to do nothing. They could hit us too hard in too many ways if we left the association. They said so without any ambiguity. The final result was that we did not modernize the plant. We could not afford to do so in the circumstances.

Did time permit I could quote many cases where trade associations, monopolies and cartels have retarded the modernisation of plant and equipment. On the other hand I could give as many cases where sharp and unrestricted competition in American industry had forced the hands of boards of directors and had compelled them to instruct their production men to install the most modern and up-to-date capital equipment without delay. The conditions under which industry operates and not the relative knowledge of their production determines whether Great Britain or the United States shall have the most ample and up-to-date capital equipment.

On the other hand some British economists and parliamentarians have joined in urging that British capital spending should be reduced in the national interest. This is where theorists so often go wrong. No nation can provide its people with the standard of living to which they are entitled without the necessary tools. British tools are inadequate to achieve that aim.

There is far too much talk in Great Britain of the need for men to work harder, faster and for longer hours if the nation is to overcome its present difficulties. It is true that there is need for some improvement in this direction. Yet better pace and longer hours are only a small part of the necessary changes. In a machine age there is far too much emphasis on brawn and far too little on machines. No matter how well men work, they cannot offset the steadily increasing American lead in machines.

INCREASING PRODUCTION

Better working pace will increase production. More and more up-to-date capital equipment for industry is capable of increasing it in far greater degree. The third factor, and sometimes it is more important than either of the other two, is the proportion of the total persons employed by a business that are engaged in actual productive work. Actually it is as important for each nation to have as large a proportion of the total population doing productive work as it is for each company. How large this proportion will be will depend on the system of management used in the case of a company and in the industrial policy and methods of the government where a nation is concerned.

In an earlier book (*Secrets of Industry*) I have recorded the percentage of non producers employed in motor car manufacturing firms in Great Britain, in the United States and on the continent. The figures obtained were from about a dozen British firms, from about six firms on the continent and three in the United States. The number of non-productive workers required for each hundred productive workers was obtained by me personally by actual count on the job, or by people in whose knowledge and judgment I had entire confidence. They were all made on the same basis.

For each hundred productive workers, the American firms used only twenty-five non-productive, the British firms an average of seventy-five non-productive and the continental firms an average of one hundred. Advertising, sales and service staffs were not included. The average of American non-productives would not have held up to so favourable a level had the average of the whole of the industry been taken, while the British and continental European firms would have shown up better had all the firms been included. This was not research undertaken on a scientific basis to compare the average efficiency of national industries. It was merely an investigation which took place in the course of my business for my own information and guidance. The differences between the different countries surprised me.

The variations between individual companies in Great Britain in the same industry were even greater. They varied from as low as 33 to 100 in one case to 140 non producers to 100 productive workers in the worst case. The period in which the investigation took place was over the ten years from 1925 to 1935. These comparisons are between firms in the same industry. It gave me striking evidence of the wastage that could and did take place in a company by the use of a wasteful system of management and administration. Experience has since confirmed that very wide variations can and do take place in other industries.

The larger the company and the greater the degree to which it is ruled in detail from the top on a figure basis, the higher will be the ratio of non productive workers required to work the system. Exactly the same is true of government. The greater the degree to which the national economy is planned and controlled from the top, the more of administrative civil servants and office staffs that will be required for that purpose. But because a national organisation is much larger, the percentage of increase brought about by these methods is considerably greater in the case of a government than it would be in an average business.

There are people who believe the increase in the production of real wealth in Great Britain since 1937 or 1938 was greater than might reasonably have been expected. The Central Statistical Office of the Government, on the basis of 1935 rates, shows that the gain in production in the twelve years from 1937 to 1949 was 22 per cent. The London and Cambridge Economic Service puts the increase over this period at ten per cent.

The Government selected 1946 as their basic year for industrial comparisons for obvious reasons. It was the country's worst year with industry disorganised in the change over from war time production to peace. Full employment in 1949 alone should have enabled production that year to have risen fully 13 per cent over 1937-1938. New tools and equip· ment had been poured into British industry faster than ever before between 1937 and 1949. The increase in the total of British production because of more and better tools should have enabled an increase in output of at least 3 per cent per annum to be made. This would give an increase of 36 per cent over the twelve-year period to which should be added 13 per cent due to full employment, or a total of 49 per cent in all. This is well below both the American and Canadian rate of increase over the same period.

Compare this with the London and Cambridge Economic Service figures of 10 per cent or the Government's estimate of 22 per cent. What happened? The system of centralised planning and controls introduced in central and local government absorbed a number of persons at least equal to a third of the unemployed in 1938. The calls of the Government on industry, the spread of central planning and scientific management in industry, the growth of larger companies and the creation of nationalised industries between them absorbed more persons in non productive posts than the total of unemployed in 1938. Other factors which will be described later, reduced the overall results to far below what the nation had a right to expect.

For none of these particular happenings were the production men of the nation directly responsible. Yet all of them affected the national production of real wealth per head and the standard of tools and equipment with which the production men were compelled to work. Copying American production technique is wise. There are other more important changes which must be made before Great Britain can be made as prosperous as it could and ought to be.

CHAPTER XI

TRAINING IN INDUSTRY

TRAINING CRAFTSMEN

Well trained craftsmen are necessary in most businesses. Some managements regard their workmen merely as hewers of wood and drawers of water, unintelligent in the mass, and often difficult to handle. Other managements regard their workers, and their craftsmen in particular, as being trustworthy and intelligent, able and willing to act on their own initiative in the company's best interests whenever the need arises. This is a fundamental point of great importance in determining the particular technique of management to be used.

If the management regard their workers as being unintelligent, difficult to handle and in addition that they are prone to act in a manner contrary to the company's best interests unless they are closely watched, then several things must automatically follow if that management be logical. They will not waste time and money in giving any more training to apprentices than the minimum that will serve their purpose. They will not bother about giving more advanced training to craftsmen. They will pick the best of their craftsmen to appoint as foremen. They will not trust the intelligence of their foremen or their reliability as an officer of the company when dealing with trade union matters. Because they do not trust workers or foremen they will use more of higher supervision and figures than necessary.

Quite logically managements which think in that way go further. Where piecework is used they take rate setting and piecework setting completely out of the foreman's hands.

They consider he would favour the workers far too much. The foreman is indispensable; but because of the belief of some persons that he lacks intelligence, someone else plans his tools for him, production methods, machine loading, output, machine and tool maintenance and other similar things. Foreman and individual workmen are held closely in line by detailed costing—on every separate piece in many factories.

Where this technique rules, management will import bright young men from the universities whom they will put over the workmen and the foremen to do those jobs which they believe require a greater amount of intelligence than they consider either the foreman or the workers possess. Very few foremen will be promoted above that level. Young men out of the offices, often with no special training, or young men who have spent some time in a technical college or university, or technical college graduates will usually be given most of the better positions within the factory for which foremen, craftsmen or semi-skilled workers would not even be considered.

It will be obvious that the technique of management referred to above is scientific management. It came as a shock to me to learn from graduates of universities and technical colleges that they had been taught that craftsmen and other manual workers are unintelligent and must therefore have their work planned for them in detail. Many graduates have told me that in the future industry will be run by the best brains in the country. The more intelligent children will be picked out from among the masses by the educationalists and given higher education. The result of this teaching that higher intelligence can be picked out with certainty by school tests, and that higher education is indispensable to promotion to the higher posts in the future often makes men with a degree scornful of the knowledge and intelligence of others who have not similar qualifications.

A wiser point of view, and one more in accord with the facts is that men of all ranks from workman to managing director may have knowledge of their jobs and intelligence well up to the standard of a university graduate. For the work many have to do, an apprenticeship is the better training. Wise managements will make that training as thorough as they can contrive, including attendance at a technical college where that is possible.

Some of the wiser firms continue training after workers have become craftsmen to keep them interested in and knowledgeable about new developments in industry. They regard their workers as trustworthy. Both workers and foremen are encouraged to act on their own initiative. Experience proves that workers are happier and work better if they are well trained and then are treated in this way. A great deal of close supervision over the workers in such circumstances is an irritation to the workers and a waste of money for the company.

Scientific management operates on the opposite belief. In many factories run on this system, no matter how often a workman may have done the same job, he will be handed an operation card or other written instruction showing in detail exactly how the job should be done, the time it should take and other information. The clerk in the office who fills in the information on the card is regarded as being intelligent. The craftsman is not. The filling in of job tickets, move cards, instruction cards and the rest of the paper work usual in factories running on this form of management, requires considerable additional staff. It costs more.

Scientific management does not stop at assuming that workers are relatively unintelligent. It assumes even more strongly that they are not trustworthy. A costly and elaborate system which is the very foundation of scientific management is introduced to ensure that there shall be no slacking. The length of time it should take a workman to do each job is calculated carefully in advance. How much time a worker takes to do his work is measured carefully against the clock to ensure that he does not take too long. He is under a microscope of close supervision. All he does is checked closely against standards of performance. Scientific management assumes that workers performance cannot be checked too closely, as to accuracy, time taken and cost per piece. These are fundamental beliefs and practices where that system is used.

American trade unions objected strongly to scientific management in the past, and rightly so in my opinion. Owing to trade union objections, individual piecework and this type of close checking of the individual worker has been done away with in most American industries. The average American worker on day work maintains a higher average output per hour under similar conditions than the average British workman on piecework. It will not require proof in detail from me that the number of non productive staff required to supervise individual piecework under the system of scientific management will be much greater than would be required on daywork using good practical management. In general the number of staff required to control output and to supervise workers is very different under these two sharply opposed techniques.

Technique of Management Taught

All management is expensive. It is a costly necessity. It is not a saleable commodity. It brings no money in. Frugal and efficient, it is a basic cost which must be borne. Whatever it costs must be added to the cost of everything made. Grandiose or unnecessarily extravagant management adds to the cost of living of the worker and the general public.

Management is not a work of art or even an exact science. It has no worth in itself. It is merely a means to an end. That is to get work done ever more cheaply and quickly.

The top managements of some large companies appear impressive. That is how some of them view themselves. Yet it is not the basis on which they should be judged. Their relative success or otherwise can best be tested at the other end—the cheapness and quality of the work produced compared with that of other similar companies.

It is the bottom end of management that matters most. That is the end of management that supervises all that the company produces in the way of saleable products. Top management constitutes the talking level. The bottom level, the foremen, converts the talk into work. The quality and the cost of the work done is the standard by which managements as a whole must be judged.

There are firms, and perhaps the great majority of firms in this country, who do not have machines, tools, handling and other capital equipment up to American standards or better. This is an even greater handicap to the nation than it is to the company concerned. The latter, owing to the lack of sharp and effective competition on American lines, may be making quite a satisfactory profit with the tools and equipment it has. The nation does not have the higher standard of living it could and would have today, were the tools and equipment of British industry, and the power to drive them, up to American standards or better. The object of making this point is to stress the fact that interests of the individual company and of the nation as a whole may be widely different on some points. This is such a case.

The majority of firms whose capital equipment is not of the best can probably show good reasons why it would not have paid them to install tools and machinery up to American levels in the past, even though it might have been in the best interests of the nation as a whole for them to have done so. This is where government past and present must shoulder the principal responsibility. It is the duty of all governments in all countries where private enterprise operates to make the conditions under which industry operates such that the national interest and the interest of the individual company is the same to as great a degree as is possible. The American Government by its policy of sharp and unrestricted competition and by its anti-trust laws made it in the interest of the individual

American company to keep its tools and capital equipment up to date. British Governments, present and future, need to study what steps they should take to bring about similar results.

SELECTION AND TRAINING OF FOREMEN

The selection of foremen is of primary importance. Get a man who is a craftsman of course, but his character is what matters most. Preferably he should be a man who has been unspoiled by the psychological teaching so common in most universities today. The best training he could have had was upbringing under Christian parents in a happy home where discipline was strict but kindly. That particular training is the best I know for enabling a man to learn how to handle other men wisely and well.

In my time I have listened to or read about many methods for handling men. In addition I have had considerable experience in measuring the performance of workers under various methods. I have been assiduous in collecting the opinions of other men as to which methods worked out best in actual shop practice. Almost without exception the opinion of men who know from actual experience is that men picked from the ranks with the same sort of education and training as the men themselves, handle men best and make the best foremen. This is as true in the United States as in Great Britain. Never in my experience have I found a university trained man or an industrial psychologist who has not trained alongside the men in the first place who makes a real success of handling men. The old methods of handling men are best regardless of all that is said to the contrary.

Men chosen as foremen under good practical management will be of better average character than university graduates. No marks are given for character in obtaining a university degree. Good character should be given preference over everything else in selecting a foreman. Knowledge of his craft or trade should come second. A sense of humour, tact and friendliness are all of them at least as important as mental brilliance. When the management selects the man the workers would have selected for his character had the workers been choosing the best man for the job, they will have made the wisest possible selection for foreman.

The methods foremen are taught and the training they receive are important to the success of any business. Scientific management was merely a label in the first place. A man who had no university training himself and who never rose above the level of superintendent in a big company, selected it as the best title he could use to sell the system of management he evolved. It was not a good system, but it was popular with the heads of the larger companies. Then the universities took it up because that system of management increased the number of posts in industry which university trained men might secure. It increased considerably their chances of securing the senior positions. Automatically it decreased proportionately the opportunities for working men to win their way from the bottom to the top.

British working men very naturally believed that, when industries were nationalised, their chances of promotion would be improved. They saw former trade union leaders with no experience in running a business and with no university degree appointed to positions at or near the top of these nationalised concerns. That appeared to constitute a precedent for promotion from the ranks.

Things did not work out that way. I have had repeated complaints by craftsmen in the various nationalised industries of young men from the universities whom the craftsmen have had to take round and teach their work. In a year or two they have to take orders from these same men. They realise that the slim chance they had of promotion from the ranks is now gone under nationalisation.

One thing British workers did expect when trade union leaders became the heads of government departments or nationalised industries was that the intelligence of the rank and file would be recognised by these persons if by no one else. Again the opposite happened. My work as a consultant in many government departments brought me in touch with many senior civil servants for whom I have the greatest respect. They have told me that some few of the representatives of the workers promoted to high places have spoken more contemptuously (in private of course) of the intelligence of the masses than any other persons who had held similar posts. With other men promotion to higher position did not change their point of view. They strove for better conditions and chances of promotion for workers. That was their reason for pressing for better education for the masses—to give the under dog a better chance. Their efforts to win promotion for themselves did not check their efforts to increase the opportunities of promotion from the ranks.

Prudent universities will not train students in one only of the various techniques of management. It is impossible to foresee what particular system of management may be in vogue in the various businesses their graduates may join. It is wiser that students should be made aware of the various methods and the principal differences between them. Unfortunately this is not done. As a rule only scientific management is taught. This is a pity. In teaching of this sort, the principles of both techniques of management should be given.

The technical colleges have done invaluable work in training apprentices, craftsmen and foremen, in the subjects industry cannot teach as competently. They are preparing to do even better in the future. There are other subjects which industry is better equipped to teach, if they will only take the trouble. It is my opinion that businesses and technical colleges working together can give apprentices and craftsmen a far better training than it is possible for either technical colleges or businesses to do working without the assistance of the other. It is also my opinion and that of many others that this training has the greatest effect when the practical and the theoretical training are taken simultaneously.

The universities, by comparison, have a much more difficult task in training men for industry. In chemistry, metallurgy, electrical research, design and for a number of other similar specialist positions in industry, a university trained man or one with a thorough full time training in a technical college is essential. On the production side generally the technical college and industry combined will usually do the better job. The universities do not have either the equipment or the practical experience that would be necessary to enable them to do the job as well.

Men with intellects and character at least as good as those of university graduates will be found on the shop floor of most businesses. If industry took the trouble to give the best of their workers a thorough training, they would do at least as well when they were fully trained as university trained men. It is often forgotten that the training of a craftsman takes years longer than the average university degree for a student intending to enter industry. Apprenticeship covers a narrower range, it is true; on the other hand it is usually much more thorough. Craftsmen are specialists in their own line. Good practical management will see to it that training is thorough and as varied as is necessary for the work they do.

TRAINING POLICY

When the top management of any company includes one or more men who have won their way up from the bottom on merit, usually they are fortunate. Such men will recognise the value of a thorough early practical training to their business career. They will work to ensure that all apprentices in their firm get a training at least as good as they received, and preferably better. They will impress on their associates the value of a thorough early training to all apprentices and that it should be continued with at least a percentage of the men at craftsmen level or higher.

Lads who are not intelligent or who are not prepared to settle down and work well should not be engaged as apprentices. Those that do not appear likely to measure up to these standards should be weeded out in the first six months. Firms cannot afford to waste time and money on training men who are not likely to make intelligent, trustworthy and resourceful skilled craftsmen.

Their skilled craftsmen are more important to the average firm than some persons realise. They are the shock troops of industry. They lead and set the standards for the other workers on the methods usual to the trade. They are always given the more difficult jobs. They set the pace. The other workers usually follow their lead.

The best of the skilled craftsmen should be watched so as to discover which of them is likely to be worthy of promotion. A few of the likeliest should be tried out on rate setting, time and motion study, plant layout, jig and tool design, production planning and similar things. It is not wise that they should be left permanently on any of these jobs. It is my experience that a year is long enough for them to get all they will need to know of these subjects if they are destined for a more senior post. More than two years is too long on specialist jobs of this sort for any man that you intend to promote. Good all round knowledge, as wide as possible, is what should be aimed at.

It is not wise just to pick a man from the ranks when another foreman is required. Several men should be tried out in the way I have described, several years before another foreman is required. Several years of training is required to train them for foremanship. The men so selected and trained should not be told they were being trained for foremanship. All that should be said is that they were being given special training to see how they develop. Those who do not make good should be dropped back into the ranks. Only those that seem suited to promotion above foreman rank should be appointed foreman. This was the method usual to the large company in which I worked. It is the method I have always used. It will produce better foremen than any other I know.

No matter how much and how good the training a man receives before his appointment as foreman, that training is not enough. Training and development should continue after they have been made foreman. They should be given opportunities to visit other factories. Foremanship should be regarded as the best training position within the company for higher posts on the production side of management. This training must be given by the more senior officers of the company in their day to day tasks. Training their subordinates should be regarded as a duty of major importance.

How well the foremen develop after their appointment will depend on the methods and point of view of their seniors and on the technique of management used. Because the universities cannot turn out skilled craftsmen or fully trained foremen, and because both are necessary to each business, scientific management introduces university and technical college graduates above foremen level. The foremen's authority under scientific management is limited. He is not encouraged to plan or act on his own initiative. His chances of further promotion are very small indeed. Senior management do not take foremen into their confidence or spend time in training them.

Under good practical management the opposite occurs. Their immediate seniors take the newly appointed foreman into their confidence in matters of company policy. Foremen are encouraged to think and act on their own initiative. This is the only way in which it can be discovered whether they have the qualities that would fit them for a more senior position. It also builds up in them confidence in their ability to carry on their duties successfully, unaided by more than an outline of policy and plans from above.

Training Works Managers

The technique in which a works manager has been trained can be determined at a glance by the number of non productive staff he requires in his office to help him run his job. As a works manager I took over the job from a man who was using a staff of twenty-five in his office to run a factory employing approximately five thousand men. I cut the number to seven and then to five. I have seen other factories using the technique of scientific management where the non productive staff employed in or reporting to the works manager was more than 125 to handle a plant employing under five thousand. In fact I took over the job of works manager in a factory employing less than two thousand men where the progress and planning staff reporting to the works manager alone numbered nearly a hundred. Using the ordinary methods of good practical management this number was reduced to less than ten. It should be added that the work in that factory was particularly difficult to control and required more than normal staff for that purpose.

The principles of good practical management are to move the planning and the decisions to be made as close as possible to the work. Actually in sight of it is preferable, as then far fewer figures are required. This means training the foremen thoroughly and giving them as much authority as possible.

Scientific management works on the opposite principle. The foreman is not considered competent to make the decisions they would normally make under good practical management. The planning of work is taken from them. Someone else will determine what job a workman will do next, on what machine and by what methods. Tools and jigs will be designed, made and maintained by others. Piecework prices will be set by someone else. Machine maintenance will be taken out of his hands. Foremen are not allowed to hire their own workmen, to impose discipline or to fire them; a personnel manager takes over that job.

Very few of the jobs normally done by a well-trained foreman on good practical management are left to him when the system of scientific management is introduced in full. The total number of foremen employed is seldom increased. The total of non productive personnel required for these new and additional specialist functions increases sharply. The works manager becomes the important man who, with a group of specialists around him, tries to plan and control everything in great detail.

In some larger companies there is a works director who has under him a works manager, a production manager and a works engineer all of roughly equal rank, each with specialised duties and reporting directly to him. Occasionally he will have a chief inspector who reports directly to him and perhaps a planning or a tool room chief as well. This will split the works into functional sections each with its own personnel reporting to one of these specialists. This is functional management superimposed on scientific management as applied to a works. A large top management on the production side such as described here is frequently applied to factories employing as few as two or three thousand employees. The rise in the number and in the average rate of reward of the number of non producers required to manage a works on this system is obviously very considerable.

There are sharp differences in the beliefs of scientific and of practical management, as to which end of management it is most important to train, how long it should take to train them and methods of training that should be used. Good practical management puts the principal emphasis on the bottom end, on training an apprentice to be a craftsman, on training a craftsman to become a foreman, and in training foremen to become works managers. The method of training is usually to give a foreman practical experience in as many different supervisory jobs as possible. Outside contacts should be used as well to make the training for works manager as wide and as thorough as possible.

In my experience it requires at least six and preferably eight years of really intensive training after a man has finished his apprenticeship before he will make a good foreman. Wise managements will shift their foremen about from one shop to another and into as many different jobs as possible before they would regard a man as sufficiently well trained to make a good works manager. Add in the four years of apprenticeship, six years of training for foreman and eight years of training for works manager and it totals eighteen years. That was the sort of training I received and about the time it took. Whenever any big business tackles the training of their foremen and works managers in this way, it must be obvious that no university can possibly give training as long, as diversified or as thorough. Doing a job or seeing it done is always better training than talking about it with men who have not done it themselves.

CHAPTER XII

TRADE UNION STUDIES OF AMERICAN INDUSTRY

AMERICAN PRODUCTIVITY

A team of British trade union officials was sent to the United States by the T.U.C. General Council in 1949. They were to report on the attitude of American trade unions toward increased productivity in industry, and on other points of interest to trade unionists. Their report is well written and interesting.* It should be widely read.

A particular feature of the report is that it is very honest and it does not hesitate to record where American trade union opinion is the effective opposite of their own. They do not use ambiguous phrases, but state facts clearly in a way that anyone can understand. The relatively few pages that deal with American industrial policy are lucid and to the point. This part of the report is of great general interest, although much of the remainder would be interesting only to trade union members. The conclusions and recommendations should be read by all business men. Although unofficial and only the opinion of the members of the team, they are an excellent guide to trade union plans and future policies.

One of the most important statements made in the report is that American trade unions do not regard high company profits as anti-social, or something to be prevented. The report goes on to state that this attitude is typical of the American unions' acceptance of a capitalist economy. In fact high profits are regarded as evidence of high efficiency and therefore of high outputs per man hour, when earned in

* *Trade Unions and Productivity*, British Trades Union Congress, 2s. 6d.

the face of really sharp and effective competition. American workers like their company to earn a high profit because they are then in a better position when they set about trying to get an increased standard of wages for themselves.

The statement is made that the American unions do not, as a rule, seek wage increases by means of nationally negotiated agreements. On the contrary, negotiations take place firm by firm. The most prosperous firm in the industry is usually tackled first. They usually secure from them a higher rate of wages than the poorer firms in the industry would find it possible to pay. The leading firm in an industry, running at a high output rate and making very large profits, is in a particularly vulnerable position to trade union attack. They are always worried at the possibility of a strike with all their competitors remaining in full production.

Less efficient firms are tackled later. In the end they usually pay the same or slightly lower rates than the more efficient firms. This British trade union team grasped the all important fact that the difference in efficiency between the best and the least efficient firm in the same industry is much smaller in the United States than in Great Britain. They add, and rightly, that as a direct result the average efficiency of American production is high.

It is important to remember that the British trade union movement, as a body with political influence and aspirations, does not believe either in the capitalist system or in sharp and unrestricted competition such as exists in American industry. It is particularly courageous, therefore, that this team should comment so frequently on the fact that American productivity is high mainly because the competition is so keen. Less efficient firms must achieve up to at least a certain standard of performance set by other firms in the industry or die.

Mobility of American Labour

The team concedes that wage rates can be forced up more successfully on the technique American trade unions use than on British methods. They give the reason. Some firms will always be more progressive than the rest. They will improve tools, methods and products, and so increase their profit ratios. Wage increases negotiated on a national basis are usually determined and set by what the poorer firms can afford to pay. At best they will not be set higher than the average of the industry can afford.

The American unions approach the most prosperous firms first. They force their wage rates up to as high a level as their profit ratios will stand. This they argue is good for the nation. It gets the average of wage rates higher than they otherwise would be. It keeps the most progressive companies under constant pressure to do even better by every means at their disposal in order to restore their profit ratios, after wage increases have been granted, to their former levels. This constitutes one of the principal spurs to American industrial progress.

American trade unions justify this technique in another interesting way. If the most efficient firms in an industry pay wage rates no higher than the poorest firms in that industry could afford, the more efficient firms would make too much money too easily. They would lessen their efforts to do better. This particular spur to greater efficiency would largely disappear.

The slightly lower wage rates paid by the less efficient firms in the industry keeps them in the race. It makes their competition with the leading firms keener than would otherwise be the case. Good handicapping can convert what would otherwise have been an uninteresting race, into the keenest and most thrilling competition of the day. The same is true of industry.

Other national advantages arise from these wage differentials.

American workers will leave their place of employment to go to some other firm that pays higher wages even if it means moving to a new locality. This is a very good thing for the country. More efficient firms paying higher wages draw workers from the less efficient, even when there is full employment. It enables a prosperous industry facing a rising demand and paying high wage rates to draw workers away from less prosperous industries where the volume of work is falling and where wages are usually lower. This is something which must be made to occur if some industries are to expand to meet the national need and to allow other industries to contract as the amount of business they have to do declines. This achieves a necessary movement of labour without direction by the state.

Nationally negotiated wage agreements prevent this movement. Wages are more or less at the same level in the efficient and the inefficient firms. They are often the same in very prosperous industries and in those that are declining. Workers out of a job often decline to move. They draw unemployment pay and try to put pressure on the government and wait for the government to come to their aid. They often request the government to try and bolster up their particular firm or industry, or to draw other industries to their district. "Depressed Area" is the name usually given when this particular situation occurs in Great Britain.

This trade union report on productivity mentions piecework and incentives. It gives figures showing that only about 30 per cent of all American operatives work under any sort of incentive scheme today. Only a small percentage of that total use piecework on the lines generally used in Great Britain today, and advocated by the T.U.C. The report neglects to say that American trade unions have had far more experience with piecework than British trade unions. They also neglect to say that, based on this longer experience, most of the American trade unions have been working with some success over the last thirty years to get it thrown out. They have succeeded in doing so in all but a very few industries. American workers in boots and shoes, garment making, and in some sections of the textile industry still prefer piecework or some other form of incentive.

Joint consultation is something else that was tried out very extensively in American industry between the latter part of 1941 and 1946. This fact is not mentioned in the report as clearly as it ought to have been. By the latter date, both sides had had enough of it. Production committees and joint consultation were discarded. Actually it is not popular in most of British industry, and it is now showing a tendency to decline. This is to be expected, judging by American experience. In spite of this fact the T.U.C. are driving for an extension of joint consultation as a means of increasing their say in the management of industry.

The British trade union report on productivity is surprisingly honest in that it says American unions do not expect or want to be consulted about the way plants should be managed. It is the considered policy of American trade union leaders to leave the job to management. They believe that American managements are competent and that they will do all that is necessary in this direction.

The report further adds that the lack of joint consultative machinery between unions and managements in the United States has not made relations between the two "distant". Their general impression was that relations were better than in many British factories. They record that American unions are not altruistic. They are out to increase production because they know it is in their own best interests to do so. They do not bother themselves with new ways of increasing productivity. They know they can rely on managements to do all that is possible or necessary in that direction.

This British trade union report records that American trade unions believe industrial performance in the U.S.A. is high because they use the capitalist system and because that system is the best and fairest that exists in the world today.

Accordingly they do their best to make it work well. British trade unionists, on the other hand, do not believe in the capitalist system. They are out to replace it with another system of their own devising. One of the greatest disappointments they could suffer would be for the capitalist system to work really well. The British public might then insist that it be retained. That would mean the complete defeat of their plans for the future. They are out to prove that capitalism has failed, that it cannot be made to work well, and that it must be swept away with as little delay as possible. It is not surprising that the capitalist system in Great Britain has not worked well under such conditions.

ANTI-TRUST LEGISLATION

This trade union team say quite frankly that they believe American anti-trust legislation has had the effect of stimulating competition. They add that it is the willingness and the ability of American firms to compete with each other sharply that has caused the rapid industrial expansion and the resulting rapid rise in their standard of living. Some of these points are put very briefly and with extreme clarity in this report. Yet in spite of all they saw, it is clear that they do not intend to profit by American trade union experience on many of these points. They prefer what they still believe to be the wiser Socialist way.

One very important point from a trade union point of view is omitted from this report. Wage increases are negatived whenever prices rise. The attitude of the government in any country towards price increases of any sort is very important. The means they use to prevent prices rising unnecessarily is important to the people of the nation as a whole. It is even more important to the trade unions in their efforts to raise the wage rates, and particularly the real wages, of the workers.

Over the last seventy years or more, successive British governments have either permitted or have openly encouraged the formation of price rings, trade associations, cartels and monopolies. The primary purpose of these organisations has been to raise and maintain prices by agreement, to allocate work and territory, and either to lessen the sharpness of effective competition or to do away with it entirely. The American Government has banned all organisations formed for such purposes, and has placed heavy penalties on actions of this sort by individuals or by companies. This action by the American Government is, in effect, a strong support of the trade unions and of the interests of the general public.

It will be said that there is monopoly legislation on the Statute Book in Great Britain today and that investigations into monopolies have begun. From the point of view of anyone with experience in American industry, this law was never meant to be more than a small appeasement of public opinion. It was not meant to work. It could not be made to work while all the government owned industries were monopolies. Monopoly is not harmless because it is owned by the state. It is usually more dangerous in its concentration of great economic power in a few hands and often less efficient in operation than monopolies in private ownership.

American experience in the matter of monopolies is ignored in this report. The British Trades Union Congress and Socialists generally prefer monopolies. Their own organisations and the nationalised industries are all designed to be run and controlled by the few at the top. There is no unpleasant competition to show up the lack of experience of many of the men they put in charge or to prevent them from being as extravagant in their methods of management as they like.

The American Congress has helped trade unions in directions not mentioned in this report. They have passed laws to give trade unions the right to organise, and to give them protection against managements which are hostile. These laws state how trade unions may set about organising in a factory or other place of business, particularly in those cases where managements object to activity of that sort. These laws define exactly what managements must do at the request of the workers. The conditions under which trade union activity may be carried on are stated clearly and are binding on both sides. As a result of these laws American workers are in a stronger negotiating position with their rights more fully established by law. These are matters in which the British public is interested and on which they have little information. A little more on this subject in the report would have been welcome.

Scientific management appears to have been well and truly sold to this team of trade union officials prior to their visit to the United States. They did not find a great deal of enthusiasm for it among American trade union officials. In fact the team formed the impression that this type of management was being "pushed" by industrial consultants in the United States, and that it was not regarded with a great deal of enthusiasm by American managements who were much more concerned with actual results than with theories of management. The report neglects to state that the methods of Taylor and Bedaux were, and still are, unpopular with American trade unionists. In spite of all these considerations, they recommend that scientific management should be used more widely in this country in the future.

General Conclusions

The British trade union team on productivity states clearly that American trade unionists believe in results, not theories. The team reports that so long as capitalism continues to deliver the goods in the way of a steadily rising American standard of living, there is no possibility of Socialism gaining many adherents in that country. American workers are aware that there is no system in use in any other country that gives workers as high a standard of living as they can obtain under capitalism.

The team, however, are critical of American trade union attitude towards Socialism, and particularly toward the new industrial, economic and social life which is being introduced in Great Britain under trade union leadership. This latter statement is taken from the first paragraph of their report. That this team of British trade unionists believe the British trade union movement to be in the lead over their American cousins on many points is clear. They indicate that they are anxious to instruct American trade unionists on the many social and political matters—in which they believe British trade union policy is better.

In these circumstances it is not surprising that they refused to be convinced that the American competitive economy works as well as American trade unionists believe. They failed entirely to get American trade unionists to understand and accept the British trade union policy of "wage restraint". Apparently the American trade unions had in mind that trade unions had been formed to raise wage rates. They did not like or understand the use of trade unions in an effort to "restrain" wage rates from rising.

It is generally accepted in trade union circles that when some trade union forces its wage rates up faster than some other union in the same country, that the union whose wage rates rose fastest was better led. Trade unionists generally are beginning to believe that the same sort of comparisons are just as valid between different countries. For example, the United States does not possess natural industrial advantages in aggregate which would justify American real wages being materially higher than British. American real wages are high mainly because of American trade unions. In such circumstances American trade union leaders think they have done the better job, and that British workers have little to be proud of in spite of the social and political activities of their leaders.

The greater the degree to which the men at the top of any large organisation take the direction, planning and control of affairs into their own hands, the larger the staff they will require for this purpose and the more its management will cost. The more the top men handle affairs in detail, the less junior executive officers will be allowed to do on their own initiative. The more the voice of the men at the top is heard, the less the opinions of those in the junior ranks will count in determining current and future policy. This is as true of trade unions as it is of big business.

American trade unions are much more democratic in their structure. Branch officers have much more power and are encouraged to act on their own initiative. Junior officials and the rank and file of the British trade union movement have much less say in day to day policy and action. They take little or no direct part in wage negotiations. Why these points were not brought out more clearly in the report it is hard to say. It might be that the members of the team knew that a report on those lines would not have been welcome to the few at the top of the trade union movement in Great Britain.

It would appear that the members of this team reported fairly what they saw. They appear to have recommended only those things they had reason to believe British trade union leaders would prefer. More power for trade union officials would not be an unfair summary of their recommendations. In spite of all they saw their recommendations imply that they came back convinced that British trade unionists have nothing worth while to learn from American unions. The present policies of British trade unions would be continued unchanged and be intensified if they have their way.

It is well known that the British trade union movement has always blamed the relative inefficiency of British industry on the lack of knowledge of British managements and on their unwillingness to take the necessary steps to put the wrong things right. This team also believes that American industrial leadership is due to the superiority of American managements. They did not stop to consider that a great deal of the apparent superiority of American managements was in fact due to wiser tactics of American unions. Had they thought that, as honest men, they would have had to recommend the adoption of some of these American trade union tactics. They did the opposite. They regard current British trade union tactics as superior to American. This team obviously felt they had little to learn and much to teach their American opposite numbers.

The principal recommendation the team makes may come as a surprise to many business men and others. It is that the British trade union movement should organise itself as industrial consultants to British industry. Joint consultation is intended to be the means of investigation and of offering advice. They do not say with any degree of precision what action would be taken if their advice were not acted upon.

As a means to this end they recommend that the title of trade union "organiser" should be changed to "production engineer". Changing the title the report says is not enough. They insist that those men should be so thoroughly trained that they should be as competent in all respects as the industrial consultants British managements occasionally employ to give them advice. The report does not say by whom this training should be given, by what methods, or how long it should take to make trade union organisers into competent industrial consultants teaching the technique of scientific management.

The unwise policies of British trade union leaders over the last forty years or more were responsible for the low standard of living and low real wages of their members relative to American workers. Had their leaders done their job properly, British workers would still be as well paid as workers in any other country. Had British trade union leaders known what to do and how to set about it, the mass unemployment between the two great wars would have been avoided. The United States would not have dominated the world industrially to the degree she does today. Great Britain with the Commonwealth, would have been almost equally wealthy and industrially quite as efficient.

This team of British Trade Union officials, far from learning that lesson, clearly felt they were in a position to teach American trade unions on many points. They came back believing that British managements must be taught and be made to do their job better in the future and that trade union leaders and organisers should be given the job of teaching them. British trade union policies in other respects will continue, if this report be implemented, on much the same lines as in the past.

CHAPTER XIII

OTHER REPORTS ON AMERICAN INDUSTRY

MANAGEMENT ACCOUNTING

Other teams were sent to the United States by the Anglo-American Council on Productivity to report on other than purely production problems. The first of these teams to report was on management accounting.

There is an indisputable tendency on the part of accountants, industrial consultants, educationalists and others to over-rate the importance of the various management techniques to industry and the nation. I recognise the tendency in myself. The report of the Management Accountancy team reveals this bias in unusual degree. Their report opens with the following "In the opinion of the team, after very careful consideration, the greatest single factor in American industrial supremacy is the effectiveness of its management at all levels."

The team bring forward no valid proof that there is foundation for their opinion. It is an obviously incorrect assumption. Management itself brings in no real wealth. American management could be more effective only if it produced better working pace, ensured that workers were provided with better tools or ensured that a larger proportion of the total of persons engaged in industry did useful productive work as a result of better management. They produce no evidence that American leadership in any of these particulars was brought about directly by American management technique. As we have seen, the evidence is that other factors are responsible for national performance on these points.

American management, like British, varies from frugal efficiency to frank extravagance according to the company and the conditions under which it operates. If you know where to look you can find in the United States small, medium and large sized companies using the most frugal and efficient forms of practical management. There are others, usually large and very prosperous companies, which use some of the most elaborate and expensive forms of scientific management.

In most of the better American factories, the efficiency of the purely productive work done will be high regardless of the particular technique of management used. The administrative side of management however may cost twice as much where management is elaborate than when it is frugal. There will usually be no direct rise in productive efficiency to show for the great rise in the cost of management itself. Wealthy men's homes usually show the extravagance usual to great wealth. Companies show the same tendency, particularly in management. Poorer companies cannot afford it. They cut their coat according to their cloth.

I read the management accountancy report carefully from cover to cover to see whether they had discovered that the cost of management, as distinct from its efficiency, varied at least as widely in the United States as it does in Great Britain. If it does so vary, then the report certainly does not say so. Quite obviously had they discovered variations they would describe what differences exist and recommend their British readers what to do and what to avoid doing in order to keep the cost of management in Great Britain low without loss of efficiency. The impression given by the report is that American management is uniformly good, frugal enough to copy as it stands, and better in all respects than British.

There is no suggestion anywhere in the report of the need for economy in the use of figures or managerial staffs. On the contrary this team, composed mainly of accountants, recommends that British industry should use more of figures and figure men. Perhaps their strongest recommendation is for the appointment of accountants to the position of controller in large British businesses with proportionately extended authority.

While much of this report is factual, wise and good reading, it has been spoiled by some recommendations that would do more harm than good to British industry. It was not the low cost and efficient performance of good practical management that caught their eye and interest. It was the more expensive and elaborate forms of scientific management found in some of the wealthiest American companies that they recommend their countrymen to copy. They recommend the type of management that caught the Russian eye—the worst and not the best features of American management. As is too frequently the case with accountants, they recommend frugality in production always, but never frugality in the use of figures and figure men.

UNIVERSITIES AND INDUSTRY

The Anglo-American Productivity Council sent out a team composed mainly of men with university degrees to report on the universities and industry. Most of them were actively engaged in higher education or were directly concerned with it. As was to be expected, this team puts in strong claims for higher education, their own speciality.

To build up their case for more men with university degrees in industry they mention that the American Institute of Management recently conducted a statistical survey of the qualifications and background of the chief executives of 204 leading American companies considered by the A.I.M. to be well managed concerns. This survey disclosed that 75 per cent of the presidents of these companies were graduates. The report stresses the fact that the A.I.M. expressed the opinion that they were surprised to find that as many as 25 of the chief executives were not university graduates.

It would be interesting to know what basis the American Institute of Management used in selecting these 204 companies. Only a very small percentage of all American company presidents are graduates. It would be impossible to prove that the more efficient American businesses were run by graduates. In fact I think it probable that the majority of the businesses picked out by the A.I.M. would be found to be run on the principles of scientific management. These are not the businesses that I would recommend British industry to copy if they wanted frugality in management as well as efficiency.

As is to be expected, this team of educationalists pressed for more men with higher education in British industry. They urge that university professors should be employed by individual businesses as consultants. They recommend that the universities and technical colleges should turn out a larger number of graduates from their full time courses. They do not attempt to prove that American industrial leadership is due to some particular technique of management taught in the universities which is different and better than the technique of management taught and used by practical men in American industry. They do not produce evidence that the United States lead is due to the greater amount of higher education in that country. Their attitude throughout is that it is a self evident fact requiring no proof.

EDUCATION FOR MANAGEMENT

The Anglo-American Productivity Council sent out a team to report on education for management. There was not on that team one man who had learnt practical management the hard way, working his way from the bottom to the top on merit. All the business men in the team had reached the top via the universities. The great majority of the team were university men. That they should press for more of higher education and in particular of education for management, was to be expected. That was the work on which, in one form or another, the majority of them were engaged.

This report gives the credit for American industrial leadership mainly to higher education and to special education for management. There is no suggestion anywhere in the report that they found anything to learn from the United States either in the American system of education or in the technique of management taught. In fact, like the trade union team, there is more than a suspicion that they thought the British system of education the best, and that British education for management could not be improved upon. In their opinion all that was wanted to put Great Britain in front industrially was much more of both. One other team looked after their own interests very well indeed.

TRAINING OF SUPERVISORS.

A team was sent out to report on American training of supervisors. In greater degree this team was composed of practical men from industry. They have turned in a better report. The following quotations from the report show how sound it is.

"The American foreman occupies the lowest rung of the supervisory ladder but he is regarded as part of the management by his superiors and is seen as such by his operatives."

"Success in handling the human material he controls is the true measure of his practical efficiency."

"Training should be done mainly within the company in terms of its own policy and practice rather than by an outside agency."

"Relatively little supervisor training, as such, is available through universities and colleges of technology."

This report is good. It would pay business men to read it. Unfortunately the men selected for this team were either interested in or were representing training establishments of some sort. Some of these were inside industry and some outside.

Once more a team did not learn anything new to teach. They brought back very little that was of value to small firms as to how to train their own staffs. Like the other teams dealing with education and training they put in a good word for the organisations in which they were interested and recommend that greater use should be made of them.

TRAINING OF OPERATIVES

One more team mainly of educationalists was sent to the United States to study the American system of training operatives. This report is a good one. It is unfortunate that it contains very little information about the many splendid apprentice training schemes operated by individual companies in American industry.

They make one strange statement. "Before the first world war the United States relied entirely upon the flow of immigrants from Europe to supply their skilled craftsmen". To my personal knowledge that statement is untrue. It was mainly unskilled and semi-skilled workers who came in, although there were undoubtedly a few skilled craftsmen among them.

There were many sound apprentice training schemes in operation in the United States and Canada long before World War I. My father was trained in such a scheme. I was trained in another. I visited several large American companies prior to 1914 to inspect their apprentice training schemes and adopted some of their best features.

Some quotations from the report follow—

"Technical and vocational schools are run on lines not widely different from those in this country. Apprenticeship was found to mean very much the same thing in America as it does in the U.K., and the training of adult workers in factories appeared to be conducted by methods similar to those at home."

"It was evident in every state visited that most vocational

and technical schools have a much more effective liaison with local industries than is usual in Britain."

"The policy of keeping the administration of vocational training in the hands of practical people clearly operated to the advantage of industry and impressed the team very favourably".

Like the others who reported on education and training they put in a good word for the sort of training establishments they represent or are interested in. They give the impression that such establishments in the United States take a larger part in the training of operatives than is actually the case. It would have been better had the report made it clear that the training of skilled craftsmen in American industry is done almost wholly by individual companies within their own organisations. That is the only place where the practical side of such training can be given as thoroughly as is necessary and at a sufficiently low cost.

Each business trains its own apprentices. The smaller companies seek the assistance of technical colleges where they are available. The larger companies employ their own technical teaching staff and give technical education on their own premises.

Each company, large and small, usually trains semi-skilled workers as they require them. Educationalists must be expected to favour training and education done within their own establishments. Operatives can be trained more thoroughly and at a lower cost within individual businesses. They are trained to the methods of the company concerned and with greater exactitude for the work they will have to do.

MISTAKES IN COPYING AMERICA

Russia copied American production methods very successfully. Russia's mistake was that she copied the theories of American educationalists rather than the actual methods of government and management used in the United States.

The most expensive and extravagant of these theories were seized on as being the key to American success and were intensified. British teams of trade union leaders, accountants and educationalists visiting the United States made the same mistake.

All the purely production teams visiting the United States came back with things they had learned, determined to do better in the future. These other teams who had more to learn, came back convinced that more of what they had been doing in the past was all that was necessary. They had learned nothing new. They used their American visit as a means to press their own claims and aims.

Other countries have copied America. Often they have copied American production methods subject to the limitations imposed by volume, design and degree of standardisation in their own country with reasonable success. On this they have superimposed their own political and trade union methods. They have then been very disappointed that the overall results were not nearly as good as they had expected.

COMPETITIVE PRIVATE ENTERPRISE

Competitive private enterprise is a practical development. It is not scientific. Few scientists like it. It irritates them. They are always trying to devise a system that will work better. So far all their efforts in this direction have been dismal failures.

The capitalist system was developed by trial and error over centuries. It has been reshaped as changing industrial conditions required it to be changed. Properly run, this system provides the highest standard of living in the world today.

Private ownership is not the most vital part of that system. Sharp and unrestricted competition is. Industrial efficiency and national prosperity are both low in all countries where competition has been killed or severely restricted. In other words countries that permit trade associations, price rings, monopolies and cartels to operate will have industries that are less efficient and people less prosperous than countries where most of these activities have been made illegal.

Real wages are highest throughout the world in the capitalist countries. Workers receive the highest wages in those countries where competition is keenest. Real wages are lower in Socialist countries. They are still lower in Communist countries.

This is something that cannot be prevented. Were the tools and methods of production equally efficient in all countries, real wages would be highest in capitalist countries where competition was keenest. The lowest level of real wages would be in the Communist countries. With production efficiency level all round, the level of real wages would be determined by the industrial system each country used.

Area, population and natural resources, do not determine the industrial efficiency of a nation. They do not determine the level of real wages that the workers will enjoy. The technique of government and the policies of the trade unions are the deciding factor. If these are wise, then wage earners will enjoy high real wages.

How well the people live is the responsibility of the nation's leaders, trade union and political; they should never be allowed to forget or evade that fact. Where real wages are low, as in Great Britain today, it is the clearest possible evidence of the folly of political and trade union policies over a long period of years in the past.

Socialism is represented as being an industrial system superior to capitalism. It is said by some persons that it produces greater industrial efficiency and gives the workers a squarer deal and higher real wages. It is interesting to trace what changes Socialism brought about in Great Britain since 1938.

Socialism as an industrial system uses the technique of

scientific management with functional management extended into the affairs of government. The planned economy and Socialism are similar terms. They are the effective opposite of competitive private enterprise with anti-trust laws as they operate in the United States. Under Socialism, monopolies and ever larger corporations are the order of the day. Controls take the place of competition.

The job of government in the last peacetime year before the war, 1938, was carried on by some 387,000 administrative civil servants. Under Socialism this figure had risen to 675,000 by 1951. The increase was not due to graft or incompetence. It was due to the installation of Socialism and the planned economy in place of competitive private enterprise.

The staffs of local government increased by about 200,000 over the same period due to the same cause. The staffs of the nationalised industries have risen by many thousands including many new additional highly paid administrative posts. Privately owned industry has had to increase their office staffs by many thousands to fill in the many new forms, to give the government all the additional information they require and to carry out their many instructions.

That the office staffs of the nation have grown enormously since 1938 is known to everyone. Many new office buildings have been built. Many stately mansions, hotels, apartment houses and other buildings have been acquired to house the rapidly growing office staffs of the nation. This is the most obvious change brought about by Socialism. It is also the most important.

The total increase in office and other non-productive personnel since 1938 in central and local government is at least 500,000. The increase in the nationalised industries is very large including a large number of newly created and highly paid administrative posts. Socialism and scientific management combined have probably increased the office and non-productive posts in industry by 1,000,000 persons.

None of these persons create any additional real wealth. They merely dissipate it.

There are very many highly paid persons filling these newly created posts. Many thousands of others are only slightly less well paid. The cost of office accommodation, motor cars, typewriters and other expenses builds up to a pretty big figure per head. The cost per head to the nation for this additional load is probably £600 per annum. One and a half million persons at £600 each works out at about £900,000,000 per annum. That is the amount Socialism cost the nation over what it should have cost on a well run system of private enterprise.

The people of Great Britain are not poor because they as a race are less capable than Americans. They are not poor because they live in a country that cannot be made as prosperous. They are poor solely because of mistakes in industrial policy made by their leaders. Were the problem to be tackled wisely and courageously by men who knew what to do and why, British production of real wealth per head could be raised to American levels in relatively few years.

Because all men like power, and because planning by the state is still popular, there will be a great temptation for those who succeed the Socialists to retain that power and to carry on much as before. That would be a betrayal of the people. The nation has a right to expect an increase in their standard of living. That requires an increase in the production of real wealth per head.

There are three ways in which this might be attempted.

1. *Faster working pace.* Lecturing the workers, incentive schemes and nationalisation have all been tried and have failed to give noticeable improvement. A change in the point of view of trade union leaders and working men that would bring a worthwhile improvement in working pace would take a long time to bring about. In other words appreciably faster working is not something that it is possible to bring about in the near future.

2. *Additional up-to-date capital equipment for industry.* This has been cut down by government decree at the present time. Even if this policy is altered, some considerable time must elapse before new and improved capital equipment in industry would raise the output per productive worker on a national basis in material degree. In other words there is no prospect of any material improvement in this direction for the next few years.

3. *Additional persons doing actual productive work.* Additional persons engaged in doing actual productive work and people working longer hours—these are the only means capable of increasing the national output of real wealth materially over the next few years. Were the people who have drifted into offices and other non-productive positions over the last fourteen years to be put to doing actual productive work instead, the national production of real wealth would rise by between 15 and 20 per cent. That would be undoing the harm done by Socialism in a way that would react to the nation's advantage. It would take a great deal of political courage to make such a move. There is none other that can be devised that would raise national prosperity more rapidly or with greater certainty.

Changes in financial policy, in government policy and regulations are effective only in the degree that they effect the three points mentioned above. Changes that leave the country with approximately the same proportions of producers and non-producers will also leave the rate of production of real wealth practically unchanged. The workers' pressure for a larger share of the real wealth produced by the nation will be pressed relentlessly. The need for both sides of industry to combine with politicians to find means of increasing the national output of real wealth materially and without delay will be overlooked. On the other hand any party that has both the knowledge and the courage to take the steps open to them to increase the British production of real wealth could put an end to the British industrial decline relative to the

United States and win the gratitude and respect of their countrymen.

TOOLS FOR INDUSTRY

The need for better tools and capital equipment for industry must not be overlooked. Better supplies of coal and of power are vital. Under private enterprise these shortages would not have lasted as long as they have in nationalised industries. Enterprise seems to be lacking as soon as the state steps in. Other countries have had the same experience.

More and better tools are supplied to industry in order to save on productive labour. These gains are negatived when non productive staffs are allowed to grow unnecessarily. The degree by which British industrial production over the last fifteen years failed to match the rate of rise in American output must be exasperating to patriotic Britons. The principal reason for its failure to rise as fast as it ought to have done has been given above. The figures that follow are startling.

If the average of British industrial production over the years 1935/1938 be taken as 100, then production in March 1951 was running at about 146/147. If American production over the earlier period be also represented as 100, then American production in March 1951 was running at about 236/237. It is clear that over the last fifteen years the rate of increase in British production was very much slower than it could and ought to have been.

Americans have usually spent more than twice as much per head as the British to modernise and enlarge their industrial tools and equipment. American capital expenditure per head between the years 1947/1949 averaged $298. Britain spent only £43 per head for the same purpose over the same period. In 1950 and again in 1951 the Americans raised their rate of capital expenditure per head. The British Government progressively curtailed the amount of capital British industry was allowed to spend over the same period. As a result the American rate of capital expenditure rose to well over three times the British rate. American industry does not have better tools by accident.

Neglect to provide the workers of the nation with tools and power to drive them up to American standards or better was not the only mistake made by the British Government in recent years. A worse mistake was to pit brawn against machines, to ask British workers to work harder, faster and for longer hours to make up for lack of adequate capital equipment and sufficient power to drive them. The "Work or Want" campaign of the late government was a mistake. It put the principal responsibility in the wrong place.

Slow working pace and restrictive tactics have limited the efficiency of British industry in the past. The lack of adequate machine tools was a far greater handicap, and one for which the workers were not responsible. The wastage of man power due to the introduction of Socialism created even greater waste. Frank acknowledgement of these mistakes would do a great deal to convince British workers the responsibility for the present situation has been put fairly where it belongs.

There are some misconceptions about government giving. The most that any government can do in normal times in the way of being generous to the people, is to give back to them some of the goods and services that they have already produced. All the apparently free services come out of the people's pockets. To enable the government to give free health and other services the ordinary folk must do without other things which they otherwise could have had. That is the essential fact.

One other unfortunate aspect of government giving must be added. Everything the government does costs more than if the same thing were done by industry or some other body. The reason is simple and obvious. The cost of administering these things by the government is higher, and usually very much higher, than businesses or charitable organisations could afford or would care to pay.

"Give us the tools" said Mr. Churchill during the war "and we will finish the job". The tools of British industry are inadequate to win the peace. They are not sufficient either in quantity or in quality to provide the British people with a standard of living at American levels or better. No steps have yet been taken that will provide the nation with adequate tools on a satisfactory scale within a reasonable period of years.

Choosing the Right System

Nations with roughly equal industrial assets within their borders do not achieve equal industrial efficiency. The technique of production is not the principal reason for these differences. How well people live is determined mainly by the political and trade union policies of the countries concerned. How great a difference exists between the different countries is shown clearly in a letter to the *Times* of 4th January 1952, written by Mr. Cyril Osborne, M.P., who gives the following figures from the United Nations Statistical Report for 1949:

Country	1949 Population	Income per capita ($)
Indonesia	80,000,000	25
China	463,000,000	27
Pakistan	51,000,000	51
India	346,000,000	57
Japan	82,000,000	100
Italy	46,000,000	235
Russia	193,000,000	308
Germany	47,000,000	320
France	41,000,000	482
United Kingdom	50,000,000	773
Canada	13,000,000	870
United States	150,000,000	1,453

This table shows by how great an amount the United States leads the world in the production of real wealth per head for the nation as a whole.

A very large proportion of the total of real wealth produced in each country is absorbed by government. Under capitalism, if the government depends on competition to keep prices low and keeps out of industry itself, this loss is at its smallest level. Under Socialism, as has been shown, the loss is very much greater. The non-productive top load which the workers of the nation have to carry under Communism is greater than under any other form of government. The differences between the living standards of different countries is given more fully in an earlier book of mine, *Politics and Poverty*.

Workers of all countries, if they are wise in their own interests, will see that the cost of administration in government is kept as low as is possible consistent with efficiency. If they investigate carefully the rival claims of the various systems, there is no doubt that they must decide that capitalism is much the better system from their point of view. The American trade unions have already made that decision. Before Great Britain is likely to achieve prosperity at the same levels, it is probable that British trade unions would have to make the same decision.

CHAPTER XIV

SECRETS OF NATIONAL PROSPERITY

PRODUCTION OF REAL WEALTH

AMERICAN production of real wealth per head in 1949 was the highest. According to the table in the previous chapter it was $1,453. Canada was next at $870. Britain was third at $773.

It might be useful to explain how these figures are obtained. An estimate is made of the total value of national production. This figure is divided by the total population of the country concerned, including men, women and children. The result is the national production of real wealth per head. This figure is sometimes taken as an indication of how well the ordinary folk, and in particular the productive workers, of a nation live. This is far from being the case.

The output of real wealth per head in the United States was about 65 per cent above Canadian levels in 1949 according to these figures. If the output of real wealth per head was a fair measure of what real wages should be, then American workers in that year should have enjoyed real wages at about 65 per cent above Canadian levels. The Canadian output of real wealth in the same year was only 15 per cent above that of Great Britain. On this basis Canadian workers would have had reason to expect real wages not more than 15 per cent above British levels.

The production of real wealth per head by the people of any country is important. This is the ultimate test of working pace, the capital equipment of industry, productive efficiency, volume and similar things. If the production of real wealth per head in the country is high, it is a clear indication that these things have been well and wisely tackled. If the people are relatively poorly paid, it is evidence that political, trade union and industrial leaders of the country concerned are maintaining policies that are industrially unwise. They are either too proud or too deeply concerned in achieving their own immediate aims to look around and learn from other nations that have done better.

Quite as important to the workers of a country is the percentage they retain of the total real wealth produced. It is interesting to compare the results in all three countries to see in which the workers fare best.

Canadian and American trade unions are affiliated. They confer. Each knows what the other is planning, and why. Both act on a considered policy. The American unions move first. Canadian wage rates move up later and sometimes much later. American money wage rates have run from 10 to 15 per cent above Canadian levels over the last 50 years, and occasionally higher.

The cost of living in Canada for working men is usually from 5 to 10 per cent below American levels. Occasionally the difference in Canada's favour is even greater. With American money wage rates running from 15 to 20 per cent above Canadian, but with the Canadian cost of living lower, American real wages run anywhere from level with Canadian to 10 per cent higher. It is significant that, in spite of the fact that American production of real wealth per head in 1949 was 65 per cent above Canadian levels, the real wages of American workers were only 10 per cent above Canadian rates. Why did American workers retain so small a proportion of the real wealth they produced compared to Canadian workers?

Convinced Socialists believe that their system gives the masses, and in particular the productive workers, a larger share of the national production of real wealth than is possible under any other system. For this reason it is particularly interesting to discover whether British workers under Socialism received a larger or a smaller share of the national real wealth produced than their Canadian cousins.

Canadian money wage rates in 1949 ran anywhere from double to two and a half times British rates. Canadian cost of living for working men probably ran anywhere from 35 to 45 per cent above British levels in that year. On this basis Canadian real wages were anywhere from 65 to 85 per cent above British levels. Many observers put Canadian real wages at about double the British levels. Whichever basis is used, it is obvious that Canadian workers got a larger slice of the national production than British workers. While the total Canadian real income per head was only 15 per cent higher than British, Canadian workers were paid some 75 per cent above British levels. Canadian workers under capitalism got a better deal than British workers under Socialism in 1949. Canadian industrial progress, however, continues at a rapid rate.

Time magazine, an American publication, is seldom flattering to Canada or to Canadian policies. In their issue of 4th February 1952, they announce that Canada has quadrupled her industrial production since 1939, and has made a great improvement in the national standard of living. The magazine gives the average income for a Canadian family of four—a man, his wife and two children, as $4,000 a year. They go on to say that this is $622 above the corresponding American average.

OUTPUT PER PRODUCTIVE WORKER

As has been said before, only actual productive workers produce the real wealth of the nation. These workers produce more real wealth in some countries than in others. Working pace does in some degree control the output per productive worker. The hours they work also affects the amount of real wealth they produce in a year. Modern production tools and methods, great volume, standardisation, ample supplies of fuel and power, are other factors which contribute to increased output per productive worker.

No reliable figures are available in any country to show how large a percentage of the total population is engaged in actual productive work. On the other hand the great majority of what are termed the working classes, are in fact, productive workers. All the upper classes and upper middle classes are non productive. A few of the lower middle class are productive while a few of the working classes are non productive.

In other words the working classes might be considered productive and the middle and upper class non productive. This enables a clearer view to be had of the facts on which national prosperity depends. Other things being equal, the larger the proportion of the working classes to the total population the greater will be the production of real wealth per head for the nation as a whole. The larger the working classes and the smaller the middle and upper classes, the greater will be the proportion of the real wealth they produce retained by the working classes.

The advantages of up-to-date capital plant and of modern production methods have not been over emphasised in this book. A large population with high purchasing power is a great national asset. So also is large scale production of relatively standard products. The United States enjoys these assets in greater degree than any other country. Because of them an average American productive worker, although working no harder or no more efficiently than a similar Canadian productive worker produces at least 65 per cent more as the figures already quoted prove. This gives evidence of the need for modern capital equipment with ample power to run it, backed up by the latest production methods. It demonstrates conclusively that a nation cannot achieve the maximum levels of production per head and prosperity without adequate capital equipment.

It is necessary to emphasise that profits paid for this superior American industrial equipment. If the profits had not been large enough, then the equipment would not have been provided on such a generous scale. On the other hand had competition not been really keen and unrestricted, much less money would have been spent on capital equipment and more would have been distributed as profits.

Capitalism does not automatically produce capital equipment on the American scale or operate it as efficiently. The British example proves that. Sharp and unrestricted competition is as necessary as ample profits if the best results are to be achieved. Neither Communism nor Socialism has produced results in the excellence of industrial equipment or in the efficiency of their operation that are as good. For reasons already given, it is not possible for them to do so in the future.

Socialists may argue that the profits of American industry were unnecessarily and unfairly large. In theory they may be right. In practice the workers fare better under capitalism not merely in spite of, but because of high profits. The share that the workers receive of the total wealth produced is and always will be greater under capitalism than under any other system. Under Communism and Socialism, the bureaucrats multiply and prosper mightily.

As the number and rate of reward of the non-producers rises in any country, the proportion of the real wealth produced by the productive workers that they are permitted to retain grows progressively smaller. The proportion of non producers in the American population and their rate of reward compared to the productive workers has risen sharply in recent years. That is why American productive workers, although producing at least 65 per cent more per head, were paid only about 10 per cent above Canadian rates.

Socialists would attempt to explain this result by saying wealthy Americans were paid too much, leaving the workers with less than their fair share. Close investigation of Canadian incomes and profits margins relative to American will show that this is not a true explanation. There is no doubt that the incomes of the wealthy are proportionately larger in the United States than in Canada. The American worker failed to do better for himself, not so much because the non producers of the nation were too highly paid, but rather because there were far too many of them.

The low Canadian ratio of non productive to productive workers has its roots in the past. The first settlers in the American colonies were persons able and willing to do actual productive work. The aristocrats and those in senior posts in Europe did not emigrate. A few of them did visit the colonies from time to time. Some of them stayed there for a few years. The well to do non producers of Europe were not prepared to relinquish the advantages they held in the Old World and face starting life again under hard conditions in the New. The office workers were not wanted in the American colonies.

Over the years this has meant a steady drain on the productive workers of Europe. Their non producers did not emigrate. The ultimate result of such a policy, continued for centuries, was a relatively high proportion of non productive workers in Europe, and a very much lower ratio in the New World.

The conditions in Canada and in the United States in this particular were very similar for many years. In time the United States became wealthy. A nation that is wealthy usually allows itself luxuries that a poor nation cannot afford. A progressively higher value is placed on what is termed "brain work". Manual work or any form of toil or sweat is looked down upon.

THE DISTRIBUTION OF REAL WEALTH

Socialism and Communism are industrial systems designed specifically to produce a fairer distribution of real wealth than normally occurs under capitalism. These political and social beliefs are most popular in countries where great wealth and real poverty exist side by side. The masses, made envious by displays of wealth and privilege, demand a larger and a fairer share of the nation's real wealth. Trade unions were created for a somewhat similar purpose. It is not surprising in these circumstances that Socialists and trade unionists in some countries should have joined forces.

Trade unionists perform a necessary function for the community. Strong and wisely led, they act to raise the purchasing power of the masses. Where the economic knowledge of their leaders is sound, they operate to increase the production of real wealth per head. They drive the business men along the road to greater production faster than they would otherwise go. Their function is to keep industry on its toes, fully employed, stretching capacity and output to meet a rising demand. Experience shows that trade unions perform these functions best and keep real wages at higher levels when they keep clear of politics.

Socialism is a political and social ideal. No fault is to be found with the latter. Unfortunately Socialism is also an industrial system or technique. In effect it is the opposite of competitive capitalism operating under strong anti-trust laws. Its central theme is that ultimately the state should own, plan and control everything. Monopolies and great corporations are the order of the day. Top management expands to a remarkable degree and lives in princely style. Governmental staffs expand rapidly. Effective competition is killed. Governmental planning and controls take its place.

Communism, as far as its industrial side is concerned, is merely Socialism carried to its logical and inevitable conclusion. The countries that are now Communist started with Socialism. The exceptions are where Communism sprang to power under the shadow and influence of a foreign power. Frequently this was brought about by a coup de force, against the wishes of the majority. This is the unpleasant militant side of Communism.

The importance to all classes of the community of strong,

well run trade unions is not sufficiently clearly understood. Real wages are high only in countries where trade unions are strong. Equally important, but even less clearly recognised is the fact that business men's profits are greatest in those countries where the trade unions are strongest.

Politics always hamper trade union action. Real wages and business men's profits are both lower in all countries where the trade unions are allied with some political party.

Trade union leaders gain when their unions enter politics; the rank and file of the movement lose.

Socialism does away with aristocrats and capitalists. Its method is to tax them out of existence. Communism does the same thing, but in a rougher way. The reason given for action of this sort is that only in this way can the real wages of the workers be made as high as they ought to be.

Under these two systems the workers are not paid real wages as high as they receive under capitalism. No matter how or by whom operated Socialism and Communism cannot be made to succeed. The bureaucrats become far more numerous and costly than the aristocrats and capitalists they replace. The total production of real wealth suffers because so many persons are withdrawn from productive into non productive posts. The more fully Socialism is put into operation in any country the lower real wages will be compared to what they would have been under a well run system of competitive capitalism.

It must not be assumed that a heavy build up of top management, highly paid executives, planners, technicians and office staffs occur only under Socialism. Similar things happen in the United States, but to a lesser degree. Scientific management, very large corporations, central planning and controls are not exclusive to Socialism. They exist also in the United States in spite of the anti-trust laws. Were it not for these laws, effective competition would have died long ago and vast monopolies run on the methods of scientific management would be the rule. In other words capitalism is by no means a foolproof system. It operates efficiently only in those countries where the state takes effective action in the interests of the public to make it behave properly.

Many of the most elaborate and unnecessarily expensive features of the Russian industrial system were sold to the Russians by American intellectuals. Scientific management, very large companies, and all the managerial trimmings with which managements of large and very wealthy companies are apt to surround themselves have been sold to British visitors as the foundation of American progress, as the result of great wealth. They have continued to grow because competition has not always been sufficiently sharp and effective to check their growth.

When I first remember it as a young man American management was as a rule both frugal and efficient. The nation has become wealthy since. The idea has grown and has been encouraged that intellectual work is more worth-while and rewarding than purely productive work. There has been a steady increase in the number of men and women entering non productive posts in the service of the government and in industry. The numbers doing actual productive work have fallen proportionately. American management is even more efficient today than it used to be. It is not always as frugal as it could be without any loss of efficiency. Government staffs are also larger than necessary.

Americans did not work harder or faster than Canadians to produce the very much higher output per head mentioned earlier. Nor was the higher American output achieved because American trade unions co-operated in greater degree than Canadian. It was simply a matter of more modern tools with more power to drive them than Canada possessed in 1949. Large scale quantity production of relatively good industrial capital equipment with plentiful supplies of cheap fuel and power gave the United States at that time tremendous industrial advantages over Canada.

In spite of these American advantages, an output per head

65 per cent above Canadian levels was a really remarkable performance. Yet in one respect the Canadian performance was even better. In spite of the very much higher American production, Canada managed to pay her workers real wages that were within 10 per cent of American levels. Why were Canadians able to pay their workers proportionately so much more generously?

Efficiency in government and in management, accompanied by frugality was the foundation of this very fine Canadian performance. Canada's principal handicap relative to the United States is a small and widely scattered population. Sound practical management and frugal decentralised government kept the proportion of non producers in the nation low. As many of the men and women of the nation as they could contrive were doing actual productive work. This was the key to good Canadian industrial performance.

Small volume, heavy transportation costs, a lack of coal through most of the country are additional Canadian handicaps. Lack of sufficient industrial capital equipment was another. Canada is only in the process of becoming an industrial manufacturing nation. Yet by 1952 Canadian real wages had risen practically to American levels. It is an example of what a nation with a relatively small population can do for its workers if it tackles the job in the right way.

A Canadian British comparison on similar lines is equally informative. Britain's industrial development in 1949 was far more extensive and better established than that of Canada. In fact Great Britain had a larger proportion of her population engaged in manufacturing than the United States. Her knowledge of and experience in industry was far greater than Canada's. Yet in spite of all these British advantages, Canada's production of real wealth per head was 15 per cent higher.

Socialism's claim is and always has been that it provides the workers a larger and fairer share of the real wealth produced per head than is possible under Capitalism. Let us see whether this statement is true by comparing what happened in Great Britain in 1949 with what happened in Canada under Capitalism.

The Canadian production of real wealth per head in 1949 was 15 per cent higher than British. If Capitalism were a better and a fairer system for the workers, then Canadian workers would have received real wages more than 15 per cent above British levels. If it could have been achieved under Socialism, British real wages should have been higher than Canadian. Actually Canadian workers in that year received real wages which at the lowest estimate were 75 per cent above British. From a working man's point of view the Canadian Capitalist system is far superior to Socialism.

The position is worth analysis in greater detail. One hundred average Canadians in 1949 produced about 15 per cent more of goods and services than one hundred average Britons. It has been shown that the proportion of non producers in each hundred of the population in Great Britain was considerably greater than in Canada. These all shared in the real wealth actually produced in Britain and at a higher average rate than the productive workers themselves. This is why the British productive workers' share of the actual real wealth produced is proportionately so much smaller than in Canada.

British productive workers have been criticised for slow working pace and low output. We know that 100 average Canadians produced 15 per cent more than 100 average Britons and that the proportion of non-producers in each 100 of the population is very much higher in Great Britain than in Canada. The proportion of the total population at work in the two countries is much the same. It follows, therefore, that the number of productive workers per 100 average Canadians must be considerably higher than per 100 average Britons. The higher output of 100 average Canadians relative to 100 Britons is mainly due to this fact.

If American and Canadian production in 1949 are analysed

in the same way, it will be found that the output of an average American productive worker in that year must have been at least double Canadian. This should not be discouraging to Canadians. Canada is going the right way about it to raise her production per productive worker to American levels or near it. The principal need is more of up-to-date capital equipment backed by a plentiful supply of cheap power.

Canada's principal activities fifty years ago were farming, forestry, fishing and mining. Manufacturing is relatively new. Canada's population increased by about 25 per cent between 1939 and 1952. The physical volume of goods and services produced almost doubled over that period. The persons engaged in manufacturing rose by 90 per cent in that time. If Canada continues in the future along similar lines her ultimate success is assured.

If Canadian workers are alive to their own best interests they will steer clear of Socialism in any form. They will not seek to copy American forms of government or management. Their own are better. They will copy and use American production machines and technique. As a general rule these are best. They will build up the capital equipment of Canadian industry. They will continue to keep low the proportion of non producers in government and in industry. If they proceed on these lines Canadian workmen can look forward to having in a few years time the highest real wages in the world.

HIGHER EDUCATION v. PRODUCTIVE WORK

Bismark decided that higher education was necessary to put Germany in front. The job was carried through with characteristic German thoroughness. By 1914 the Germans were easily the most highly educated nation in the world.

This education was not designed merely to improve the understanding and enjoyment of life of the people. It had a much more practical object. A first step was to recruit to the service of the German Government the best brains in the country and to offer them worthwhile careers. As a means to this end the German Government offered each year to the top graduates from several of their leading universities worthwhile government posts subject only to favourable reports on their characters.

German industry followed a similar course. It was almost impossible to obtain a worthwhile position in the larger German businesses without an appropriate university degree. These moves were accompanied by a tremendous expansion in German industry. Good industrial capital equipment was backed up by excellent design, skilled industrious German craftsmen and excellently finished products.

Labels of Communism, Socialism and Capitalism or even of right and of left are allowed to cloud political and industrial issues. The universities in all countries teach much the same principles of administration in government and management in industry. Where university professors and graduates are in a position to advise and direct the industrial policies of government and business in a country, their advice in the main is the same regardless of whether the politics of the country concerned are of the right or the left. These similarities can be seen if the industrial policies of the government of the German Emperor prior to 1914 are compared with those of the Socialist government of Great Britain from 1945 onwards.

The first move in Germany was for more education, and particularly higher education. The second was the displacement of practical men from the higher positions in the civil service and the larger businesses by men trained in the universities. An era of high level planning in government and in industry began. Big businesses were believed to be more efficient than small ones. Big businesses were therefore encouraged and assisted to grow bigger. Monopolies were encouraged and developed.

Sharp and unrestricted competition was not liked. The

cartel grew rapidly, encouraged by the State. The international cartel followed. These moves and the ideas behind them produced the tremendous bureaucracy in government and in industry that is typical of Germany, even today.

Central planning by the state, scientific management, cartels, monopolies, large units, run preferably by men with university degrees were common features of the German programme and of British Socialism. The final result has been much the same in each case. The industrial efforts of both nations were handicapped by having to carry non-productive staffs in government and in industry that were far too large and costly. Said in another way, the numbers and the rate of award of the German middle and upper classes rose rapidly. The German productive force remained smaller and more poorly paid than it should have been. A similar situation has developed in Great Britain due to the adoption of the same policies.

The sons of the well-to-do in Britain today, like similar young men in many countries, regard toil and sweat as something to admire and emulate only when it is a matter of mountain climbing, winter sports, track events, athletic competitions and games of all sorts. When they enter industry they try to avoid toil and sweat in any form. They prefer to put their feet under a desk and relax. Leadership in craftsmanship is something to which few of them aspire. Yet if a movement back to productive work is to materialise, perhaps the best way to bring it about would be to ensure that it was led by the sons of the men who had made their money in industry.

Great Britain is giving higher education to a rapidly increasing number of young men and women. This is being done in the widely held belief that this is the sure road to greater national prosperity. It is surprising how wide are the national differences of opinion on that subject. Canada, New Zealand and Australia do not prefer these highly educated young men and women as immigrants. They

173

prefer persons who have learned a trade and are willing and anxious to do productive work. That these three countries pay higher real wages to their workers than Great Britain is able to do today is largely due to their preference for productive workers over those who, perhaps because of their education, are not prepared to take employment in rougher but essentially productive fields. This policy has been consistently maintained by all three Commonwealth countries over the years.

It is not enough to keep the proportion of productive workers high among immigrants entering the country. It is necessary to keep the proportion of producers high within the country. This can be done only if a large proportion of the young persons leaving school go in for productive work.

The three Commonwealth countries referred to have the advantage here. Skilled craftsmen and others doing actual productive work tend to look down on office workers. This feeling, although not nearly as strong as it was thirty years ago, makes it easier to keep the proportion of productive workers high.

The opposite situation exists in Britain. Office work is held to be socially superior. The hours are shorter and pay is better. This bad situation is now being made worse. School children are being taught that all the better jobs will go in the future to those who stay at school a year or two longer or go to a university.

This action will inevitably further check the flow of young persons into productive work and make them seek nonproductive jobs instead. Children are being taught that only the duller children should go in for productive work in the future. These, it is added with emphasis, will not be promoted. The higher jobs are to go to the graduates of the universities, technical colleges, and the higher schools. Nor is this heard only in schools. It is true of the universities as well.

Higher education is important. A sense of proportion is even more important. A high proportion of the total population doing actual productive work is essential to a high standard of real wages in any country. This is a fact that is seldom taught in schools, technical colleges and universities in Great Britain. Why is it consistently neglected?

The long summer vacation with relatively short ones at other times give Canadian and American universities a considerable advantage. Many universities insist on field or practical work in the long vacation. Professors and teaching staffs emphasise the need for practical work—for learning to do a useful job of work with their hands. It is more difficult to do with the British university vacation system. Also British professors concentrate in greater degree on high academic performance. They are not concerned about the practical side.

There is an old saying in the Bible that if a man will not work, neither shall he eat. Individuals may manage to evade that law. Nations cannot. How good their tools and how well they work will determine how much wealth per head they will produce. How well they eat and live is largely determined by the number of non producers they have to feed and support.

THE TECHNIQUE OF PROSPERITY

This book has not been written with a political aim. Socialism and Communism have been criticised, but not on social or political grounds. The industrial system or technique on which both are founded is unsound. It cannot be made to operate efficiently. The planning and control staffs essential to its operation are far too large and costly. Top heavy non productive staffs in government and in industry make prosperity at high levels impossible for any nation unwise enough to adopt either of these systems.

Some of the most mistaken theories of industrial Socialism

appear to have originated in the United States. That does not make them any less damaging to industrial prosperity. Great wealth always brings with it ideas that tend to lower the overall efficiency of businesses under Capitalism. Great Britain did very well until she became very wealthy. The United States is now beginning to make some of the same mistakes. More unfortunate from a British point of view is that some of these latest American industrial handicaps have been pointed out to British visitors as the key to American industrial leadership.

Competition has values that are seldom mentioned. Fair and keen competition is the means British sport has always used to discover the best man, the best team and the best technique. Sport has spread from Britain all around the world—all of it still based on British concepts of keen competition and fair play. That is what keeps it alive and popular.

It has the same value in industry. It is the only effective means of discovering the best and of compelling efficiency. In monopolies and very large companies, only the ideas of the men at or near the top are likely to get a hearing and a trial. Such conditions handicap industrial progress.

There is no desire on my part to criticise or belittle higher education nor to depreciate the advantages of a university education for persons entering industry. The value of these things is unquestionable. All values are relative however. In an effort to bring about a better appreciation of the value of higher education, the importance of keeping a large proportion of the population engaged in productive work has been overlooked. All classes of the British population are paying heavily in loss of prosperity for that oversight.

All that it is desired to do here is to point out the handicap to a nation that occurs when the proportion of non producers is too high. Were the British ratio as low as that of Canada today, British real wages could be as high as Canadian. To bring the capital equipment of British industry up to American levels or better would be an exceedingly costly task that would take many years to accomplish in full. The only way in which the real wages of British workers can be raised to Canadian levels in a reasonable period of years is to get the proportion of non producers down and the number of actual producers up as quickly as possible.

By all means press on with more university education for industry. On the other hand let what is taught be more practical in the future. Much more attention should be paid to non productive ratios in businesses and in the nation as a whole than has been given this important subject in the past. Industrialists have misled the teaching staff at the universities by furnishing them with statistics in which salaried persons only were shown as non productive and all wages personnel as productive. This is absurd. There are businesses on both sides of the Atlantic where there are more non producers than actual producers among wage earners.

Not merely university professors, but also business men and politicians should study the means by which non productive ratios can be kept low in government and in industry. Firms on both sides of the Atlantic have developed a technique which enables them to keep non productive ratios low without any loss in overall efficiency. In fact in the majority of cases productive efficiency has risen on the more frugal system. Some of the principal points in this technique have been given in this book.

The matter is one of urgency. National progress in the direction of lower costs and a greater volume of production brought about by the transfer of persons from non productive to productive work must be dependent in considerable degree on the progress made by individual companies. Obviously a heavy cut in government staffs is necessary before very great progress is made. Proportionately as the government cuts its non productive administrative staffs, businesses can cut theirs.

Governmental controls, regulations and decisions still prevent businesses from getting many necessary things done quickly. The art of good management has been said to be the art of giving sound decisions quickly. This is just as true of government. There is room for a great improvement in this direction in Britain.

A variety of new methods in government and in management have been put forward during the last forty years. Many have been tried out thoroughly in the different countries of the world. Workers in countries where real wages are low are unwise if they remain satisfied with things as they are. Better is possible, but only under a different system. It is the system in the end that determines how high real wages will be.

There are many well tried and proven systems to choose from. Why be satisfied with anything other than the best? The best system from a worker's point is the one that pays the highest real wages. It is also the best from the point of view of all other classes in the community. It is foolish for the people of a nation to remain poor solely because they do not insist on the adoption of a system capable of producing for them the highest attainable levels of prosperity.

The solution lies largely with the Trade Unions. Had their leaders done their job properly, British workers would still be as well paid as workers in any other country.